Hunt for Worthing ~~Inspector~~

Tribute ~~to popular~~ **popular
Lichfield cat dies**

**COWS ON THE
RUN AFTER
TRACTOR
THEFT**

Woman found in Germany

**Exhaustion blamed for
Hertfordshire fish death**

**Horsham coat hanger
theft – verdict**

...And Other *World Exclusives*
from Britain's
Finest Local Newspapers

VIKING

Published by the Penguin Group
Penguin Books Ltd, 80 Strand, London WC2R 0RL, England
Penguin Group (USA) Inc., 375 Hudson Street, New York, New York 10014, USA
Penguin Group (Canada), 90 Eglinton Avenue East, Suite 700, Toronto, Ontario, Canada M4P 2Y3
(a division of Pearson Penguin Canada Inc.)
Penguin Ireland, 25 St Stephen's Green, Dublin 2, Ireland (a division of Penguin Books Ltd)
Penguin Group (Australia), 250 Camberwell Road, Camberwell, Victoria 3124, Australia
(a division of Pearson Australia Group Pty Ltd)
Penguin Books India Pvt Ltd, 11 Community Centre, Panchsheel Park, New Delhi – 110 017, India
Penguin Group (NZ), 67 Apollo Drive, Rosedale, Auckland 0632, New Zealand
(a division of Pearson New Zealand Ltd)
Penguin Books (South Africa) (Pty) Ltd, 24 Sturdee Avenue, Rosebank,
Johannesburg 2196, South Africa

Penguin Books Ltd, Registered Offices: 80 Strand, London WC2R 0RL, England

www.penguin.com

First published 2011
1

Copyright © Penguin Books, 2011

Set in Akzidenz Grotesk and Plantin
Typeset by Estuary English
Printed in Great Britain by Clays Ltd, St Ives plc

A CIP catalogue record for this book is available from the British Library

ISBN: 978–0–241–95217–7

To everyone who keeps local news alive

Contents

Politics

UPDATE

Mayor is ousted by mice

A MAYOR has been forced to resign after mice were blamed for the loss of lager and soft drinks worth £6,200 from the community bar he ran.

The alcohol, equivalent to 120 barrels of lager, was said to have leaked away after rodents chewed through beer pipes at the Birchmeadow Centre, in Broseley, Shropshire.

But members of the town council passed a vote of no confidence in Mayor Ian McClelland, aged 54, and called for a police investigation.

Mr McClelland had acted as licensee of the council-owned community centre for 18 months, with the help of his wife Joy, 43, also a councillor.

The beer was discovered missing last month, and police launched an inquiry, but officers failed to find any evidence of theft.

Mr McClelland said: "This council clearly has no confidence in me."

Mayor is ousted by mice

A MAYOR HAS been forced to resign after mice were blamed for the loss of lager and soft drinks worth £6,200 from the community bar he ran.

The alcohol, equivalent to 120 barrels of lager, was said to have leaked away after rodents chewed through the beer pipes at the Birchmeadow Centre, in Broseley, Shropshire.

But members of the town council passed a vote of no confidence in Mayor Ian McClelland, aged 54, and called for a police investigation.

Mr McClelland had acted as licensee of the council-owned community centre for 18 months, with the help of his wife Joy, 43, also a councillor.

The beer was discovered missing last month, and police launched an inquiry, but officers failed to find any evidence of theft.

Mr McClelland said: 'This council clearly has no confidence in me.'

Fence 'illegal' (From South Wales Argus)

ARCHIVE - THURSDAY, 20 APRIL 2006

Fence 'illegal'

THE legality of fencing erected on common land in the Wye Valley is being disputed by the Open Spaces Society.

New fencing was installed on Whitelye Moor near Trellech in 2003, but the society believes that this work doesn't have the necessary authorisation from the Welsh Assembly Government.

The case is being used by the society's campaigners in their bid to highlight their concerns of erosion and exploitation to Members of Parliament as they debate the problem in the House of Commons, last night.

Owen Morgan, the Open Spaces Society's Monmouth-shire correspondent said: "Common land is, by its nature, open land and efforts to create boundaries with fencing should be prevented as this action destroys the characteristics of the area.

"Whitelye Moor is one of this area's greatest assets and should not be developed. The public has the right to walk on every common, and encroachments like these prevent us from enjoying our rights."

Kate Ashbrook, the society's general secretary: "This Bill could provide a last chance to protect our precious commons from encroachment and neglect."

Although the law currently requires anyone wishing to erect a fence, building or other work on a common to obtain the consent of the Welsh Assembly Govern-ment, too often this law is ignored.

This means that countless commons are degraded by unlawful fencing, buildings, car-parks and other paraphernalia.

Jenny Lewis, Monmouth-shire County Council's Area Manager said: "The gateway fencing and notice boards, erected three years ago, was at the request of Trellech United Community Council and the commoners' and were introduced to encourage greater access to the common and to facilitate visitor parking."

Ann Webb, clerk to Trellech United Community Council visited the area yesterday and believed that unauthorised additional fencing had been erected on Whitelye Moor and has asked the local authority to carry out a survey of the area.

The society is campaigning to persuade MPs to amend the bill, making it easier for action to be taken against unlawful works and provisions allowing local people being able to serve a notice on the local authority, forcing them to take action.

"If the Bill is not amended, it will be a lost opportunity for common land. Commons legislation was last introduced 40 years ago. It would be disastrous to have to wait another 40 years to save our commons from erosion and abuse. They are too valuable to lose," added Ms Ashbrook.

Print   Email   Share

Fence 'illegal'

THE LEGALITY OF fencing erected on common land in the Wye Valley is being disputed by the Open Spaces Society.

New fencing was installed on Whitelye Moor near Trellech in 2003, but the society believes that this work doesn't have the necessary authorisation from the Welsh Assembly Government.

The case is being used by the society's campaigners in their bid to highlight their concerns of erosion and exploitation to Members of Parliament as they debate the problem in the House of Commons, last night.

Owen Morgan, the Open Spaces Society's Monmouthshire correspondent said: 'Common land is, by its nature, open land and efforts to create boundaries with fencing should be prevented as this action destroys the characteristics of the area.

'Whitelye Moor is one of this area's greatest assets and should not be developed. The public has the right to walk on every common, and encroachments like these prevent us from enjoying our rights.'

Kate Ashbrook, the society's general secretary said: 'This Bill could provide a last chance to protect our precious commons from encroachment and neglect.'

Although the law currently requires anyone wishing to erect a fence, building or other work on a common to obtain the consent of the Welsh Assembly Government, too often this law is ignored.

This means that countless commons are degraded by unlawful fencing, buildings, car parks and other paraphernalia.

Jenny Lewis, Monmouthshire County Council's Area Manager said: 'The gateway fencing and noticeboards, erected three years ago, were at the request of Trellech United Community Council and the commoners, and were introduced to encourage greater access to the common and to facilitate visitor parking.'

Ann Webb, clerk to Trellech United Community Council, visited the area yesterday and believed that unauthorised additional fencing had been erected on Whitelye Moor and has asked the local authority to carry out a survey of the area.

The society is campaigning to persuade MPs to amend the Bill, making it easier for action to be taken against unlawful works and provisions, allowing local people being able to serve a notice on the local authority, forcing them to take action.

'If the Bill is not amended, it will be a lost opportunity for common land. Commons legislation was last introduced 40 years ago. It would be disastrous to have to wait another 40 years to save our commons from erosion and abuse. They are too valuable to lose,' added Ms Ashbrook.

Visit our website www.thisiseastriding.co.uk

HULL: Mum in court will defend refusal to pay litter fine

I'll fight council over sausage roll

in short

Hull City Council is taking a young mother to court after she refused to pay a littering fine.

By KEVIN SHOESMITH

k.shoesmith@mailnewsmedia.co.uk

A MOTHER who claims she was fined £75 for dropping a piece of her child's sausage roll is being taken to court after refusing to pay.

Sarah Davies says she hopes to persuade city magistrates to quash the "ridiculous" fixed-penalty notice.

Miss Davies, 20, of Beverley Road, Hull, was left seething after being given the fine by Hull City Council's environmental crime unit on April 21.

Now, she has received a letter, instructing her to attend Hull Magistrates' Court on June 24.

Along with the letter, signed by Nathan Chester, the authority's director of corporate governance and monitoring officer, are photocopies of notebook entries made by the litter warden.

Miss Davies says she is determined to fight the case and is demanding the warden be present during the hearing so she can thoroughly quiz him over his decision.

The offence of littering flouts section 87 of the Environmental Protection Act 1990.

Miss Davies is said to have committed the offence outside Hull Central Library, moments after she and her four-year daughter Chloe bought a sausage roll from a bakery.

She accepts a "bite-sized" piece of sausage roll dropped on to the pavement after she missed her daughter's mouth.

But in the letter she has received, the council states the fine was issued because a paper bag was dropped on to the ground.

A notebook entry, signed and dated on May 8 by litter warden Steven Hewson, states: "As I observed Miss Davies, I saw her deliberately throw a piece of paper (food packet) on to the ground and leave it."

The Mail photographed Miss Davies and her daughter with the paper bag soon after the fixed-penalty notice was issued.

She said despite offers from others to pay the fine on her behalf, she is refusing to accept it on a point of principle.

Today she said: "I decided not to pay the fine because I should never have got it in the first place.

"You shouldn't be fined for accidentally dropping a piece of sausage roll. It's ridiculous."

Miss Davies claims the piece was eaten by pigeons by the time the council official had issued the ticket.

Hull City Council employs six officers to enforce their "zero-tolerance" policy on littering.

The team works both overtly and covertly using CCTV cameras.

Anyone caught dropping litter and issued with a fixed-penalty ticket has 14 days to pay. Failure to pay can lead to prosecution and a fine of up to £2,500. Failure to pay a court fine can lead to imprisonment.

A spokeswoman for Hull City Council said: "We have disclosed the evidence to the defendant. There will be a preliminary hearing on June 24."

The council was unable to say how much the court case will cost the taxpayer.

Link

Hull City Council
www.hullcc.gov.uk

'RIDICULOUS': Sarah Davies with four-year-old daughter Chloe

PICTURE: Peter Harbour

I'll fight council over sausage roll

A MOTHER WHO claims she was fined £75 for dropping a piece of her child's sausage roll is being taken to court after refusing to pay.

Sarah Davies says she hopes to persuade city magistrates to quash the 'ridiculous' fixed-penalty notice.

Miss Davies, 20, of Beverley Road, Hull, was left seething after being given the fine by Hull City Council's environmental crime unit on April 21.

Now, she has received a letter, instructing her to attend Hull Magistrates' Court on June 24.

Along with the letter, signed by Nathan Chester, the authority's director of corporate governance and monitoring officer, are photocopies of notebook entries made by the litter warden.

Miss Davies says she is determined to fight the case and is demanding the warden be present during the hearing so she can thoroughly quiz him over his decision.

The offence of littering flouts section 87 of the Environmental Protection Act 1990.

Miss Davies is said to have committed the offence outside Hull Central Library, moments after she and her four-year-old daughter Chloe bought a sausage roll from a bakery.

She accepts a 'bite-sized' piece of sausage roll dropped on to the pavement after she missed her daughter's mouth.

But in the letter she has received, the council states the fine was issued because a paper bag was dropped on to the ground.

A notebook entry, signed and dated on May 8 by litter warden Steven Hewson, states: 'As I observed Miss Davies, I saw her deliberately throw a piece of paper (food packet) on to the ground and leave it.'

The *Mail* photographed Miss Davies and her daughter with the paper bag soon after the fixed-penalty notice was issued.

She said despite offers from others to pay the fine on her behalf, she is refusing to accept it on a point of principle.

Today she said: 'I decided not to pay the fine because I should never have got it in the first place.

'You shouldn't be fined for accidentally dropping a piece of sausage roll. It's ridiculous.'

Miss Davies claims the piece was eaten by pigeons by the time the council official had issued the ticket.

Hull City Council employs six officers to enforce their 'zero-tolerance' policy on littering.

The team works both overtly and covertly using CCTV cameras . . .

St Ives boy eats eclairs with PM

A BUDDING AUTHOR from St Ives took afternoon tea and eclairs with the Prime Minister after his *Alice in Wonderland*-style story came second in a national fiction writing competition.

Friedrich Berg, aged nine, was a runner-up in the eight to 11-year-old category of the contest, organised by *Take a Break* magazine.

He was praised by Gordon Brown after wowing judges with his story, 'The Kid Market' – a dark, fantasy tale of a child who falls down a manhole and emerges in a bizarre supermarket which sells children.

'I was very excited – Downing Street was really cool and Gordon Brown was nice,' he said.

The impossible

The St Ives junior school pupil said he often liked writing about 'the impossible', like objects coming alive and aliens.

'I wondered how it would be to be poked and prodded like a vegetable as I went around the supermarket once, and it inspired me to write this story,' he added.

The judging panel, chaired by author Anthony Horowitz, said the story was 'an absolute delight' describing the young writer as 'fresh and funny, with an imagination and sense of the absurd worthy of Roald Dahl himself.'

The competition was open to those between eight and 18 years old and attracted more than 2,000 entries.

Winners received Apple Mac-Books and £1,000 worth of books for their schools.

First place in each category and runners-up received WH Smith vouchers, publication of their stories and an overnight trip to London.

Gordon Brown congratulated the youngsters, saying he was extremely proud of what they had done.

'You have been brilliant and you should keep writing and keep entertaining,' he said.

Mum Rachel said that, despite all the famous people around and the buzz of Downing Street, Friedrich had seemed totally unfazed.

Chocolate eclairs

'He settled down on a chair in the corner with a plate of chocolate eclairs and his newly signed copy of Mr Horowitz's book and began reading.'

She says Friedrich, who is bilingual on account of his German father, Karsten, has always been a prolific reader...

Sunderland Echo

You are here News

Hitler: his part in our town fall

Sponsored by LUMLEY CASTLE

Friday 17 June 2011

Published on **Friday 13 May 2005 14:16**

Wearside Echoes with Carol Roberton Photographic exhibition shows how Luftwaffe bombs changed Sunderland for ever

THE way in which Hitler cleared the way for postwar redevelopment in Sunderland is brought sharply into focus in an exhibition to mark the end of the Second World War.

The face of the old town was changed for ever by the devastation wrought in a series of bombing raids over four years.

At the end of it, Sunderland was listed as one of the seven most heavily bombed towns and cities in Britain.

The Luftwaffe's targets were the shipyards, engineworks, the pit and other heavy industry along the river banks, and the docks and port. Although some damage was done, production was scarcely affected – the bombs having fallen instead on homes and shops, churches, cinemas and other public buildings.

The exhibition, at Monkwearmouth Station Museum until the end of August, has been compiled in conjunction with Sunderland Photographic Association and the Echo.

It includes official photographic records, contemporary news pictures of people clearing up after the damage, and atmospheric shots showing shells of buildings and bomb sites.

And alongside all of these are pictures taken this year of the same sites today, so that even Wearsiders too young to remember the Victoria Hall, St Thomas's Church, Bright Street Chapel, or the original Binns stores on each side of Fawcett Street, can clearly pinpoint them and relate to the present scene.

Martin Routledge, social history specialist for Sunderland Museums, said: "People's lives were affected in many ways during the war.

"Mostly it was having to deal with loved ones being way from home or dealing with shortages. It changed people's lives and the face of Wearside for ever."

The display is one of the ways in which the museums service is marking the 60th anniversary of the end of the war.

The current exhibition on the great graphic artist Abram Games includes wartime recruitment posters and exhortations to be vigilant and ever on the watch for traitors, with posters like Your Talk May Kill Your Comrades.

And next month a major touring exhibition from the Imperial War Museum – Their Past Your Future – comes to Sunderland Museum. Running from June 15 to July 24, it explores issues such as conflict and citizenship, while finding out about specific events. It includes a wide range of activities for all ages, personal stories and remembrances.

The exhibition has been developed from personal stories that reveal how wartime experiences changed people's lives and how they remember those they lost. It includes diaries, letters and poems – some of which are previously unpublished.

The Imperial War Museum's archives have also been explored to find unseen

footage and photographs for an audio-visual display. It will also be relevant

to the region as it includes Luftwaffe bomb maps of the area.

Hitler: his part in our town fall

THE WAY IN which Hitler cleared the way for postwar redevelopment in Sunderland is brought sharply into focus in an exhibition to mark the end of the Second World War.

The face of the old town was changed for ever by the devastation wrought in a series of bombing raids over four years.

At the end of it, Sunderland was listed as one of the seven most heavily bombed towns and cities in Britain.

The Luftwaffe's targets were the shipyards, engineworks, the pit and other heavy industry along the riverbanks, and the docks and port. Although some damage was done, production was scarcely affected – the bombs having fallen instead on homes and shops, churches, cinemas and other public buildings.

The exhibition, at Monkwearmouth Station Museum until the end of August, has been compiled in conjunction with Sunderland Photographic Association and the *Echo*.

It includes official photographic records, contemporary news pictures of people clearing up after the damage, and atmospheric shots showing shells of buildings and bomb sites.

The Imperial War Museum's archives have also been explored to find unseen footage and photographs for an audiovisual display. It will also be relevant to the region as it includes Luftwaffe bomb maps of the area.

FACTORY CREATES FOUR JOBS

Lord Mayor's trousers fall down at children's event

Lib Dems in U-turn over Exeter toilet closures

NEW SHOP WILL BRING TWO MORE JOBS TO WELLESBOURNE

Crime

Window smashed – by Easter egg

VANDALS smashed a window of a house at Kenilworth Avenue, Harrogate, by throwing an Easter egg at it.

Anyone with information about the incident, which happened between 7.30pm and 8.30pm on Friday, April 14, should contact North Yorkshire Police on 0845 6060247 or Crimestoppers on 0800 555111.

Window smashed – by Easter egg

VANDALS SMASHED A window of a house at Kenilworth Avenue, Harrogate, by throwing an Easter egg at it.

Anyone with information about the incident, which happened between 7.30pm and 8.30pm on Friday, April 14, should contact North Yorkshire Police or Crimestoppers.

Church window nearly smashed

Northend Thistle football players on the Ormidale pitch last week held their breath last Friday as a wayward shot at goal from Ben Tattersfield sailed through the air towards the stained glass windows of Brodick Church. The strike could have made a costly dent in the Northend club's kitty, not to mention a disastrous bit of damage to the Church. But thankfully the ball struck the surrounding sandstone frame and bounced harmlessly to the ground.

Church window nearly smashed

NORTHEND THISTLE FOOT-BALL players on the Ormidale pitch last week held their breath last Friday as a wayward shot at goal from Ben Tattersfield sailed through the air towards the stained-glass windows of Brodick Church. The strike could have made a costly dent in the Northend club's kitty, not to mention a disastrous bit of damage to the church. But thankfully the ball struck the surrounding sandstone frame and bounced harmlessly to the ground.

Tuesday, 10 March, 2009 **South Wales Echo**

WalesOnline.co.uk

Man is jailed for axing neighbour's noisy door

Constant creaking 'drove him mad'

Liz Keen
echo.newsdesk@walesonline.co.uk

A MAN was jailed for six months after becoming so angry about his neighbour's creaking door that he smashed through it with an axe.

Stephen Marston told Cardiff Crown Court yesterday he had complained time and time again to Paul Jones about the noise coming from his door in their block of flats in Trowbridge Green, Cardiff.

Then, five minutes after returning home at around midnight on February 5, Mr Jones, who lived downstairs from Marston, heard two loud bangs on his door and found a hole through it.

He opened it to see Marston holding an axe in one hand and a machete in the other.

The court heard Marston was waving the weapons round, saying: "I'm going to kill someone in a minute; I'll chop them up."

Mr Jones was said to have frozen in fear.

Richard Evans, prosecuting, told the court: "Mr Jones heard two loud bangs at his door and saw two large holes in it.

"He opened the door and Marston was standing outside with an axe.

"Marston said: 'That door is banging, when are you going to fix it?'

"Marston was waving the axe and machete around saying 'I'm going to kill someone; I'm going to chop someone up.'"

When police arrived, Marston, 43, told them he was suffering from depression and that the squeaky door downstairs was driving him mad.

"It was a momentary explosion of anger borne out of frustration" said defence barrister Heath Edwards.

Mr Edwards said Marston, whose long criminal record includes a six-year jail term for robbery, had trouble with his anger and has since sought counselling for it.

Jailing him for six months, Recorder Gregory Treverton-Jones QC said: "It must have been terrifying for others living in the flats."

Marston had admitted possessing weapons, causing criminal damage and using threatening behaviour.

Man is jailed for axing neighbour's noisy door

By Liz Keen

A MAN WAS jailed for six months after becoming so angry about his neighbour's creaking door that he smashed through it with an axe.

Stephen Marston told Cardiff Crown Court yesterday he had complained time and time again to Paul Jones about the noise coming from his door in their block of flats in Trowbridge Green, Cardiff.

Then, five minutes after returning home at around midnight on February 5, Mr Jones, who lived downstairs from Marston, heard two loud bangs on his door and found a hole through it.

He opened it to see Marston holding an axe in one hand and a machete in the other.

The court heard Marston was waving the weapons round, saying: 'I'm going to kill someone in a minute; I'll chop them up.'

Mr Jones was said to have frozen in fear.

Richard Evans, prosecuting, told the court: 'Mr Jones heard two loud bangs at his door and saw two large holes in it.

'He opened the door and Marston was standing outside with an axe.

'Marston said, "That door is banging, when are you going to fix it?"

'Marston was waving the axe and machete around saying, "I'm going to kill someone; I'm going to chop someone up."'

When police arrived, Marston, 43, told them he was suffering from depression and that the squeaky door downstairs was driving him mad.

'It was a momentary explosion of anger born out of frustration,' said defence barrister Heath Edwards.

Mr Edwards said Marston, whose long criminal record includes a six-year jail term for robbery, had trouble with his anger and has since sought counselling for it.

Jailing him for six months, Recorder Gregory Treverton-Jones QC said: 'It must have been terrifying for others living in the flats.'

Marston had admitted possessing weapons, causing criminal damage and using threatening behaviour.

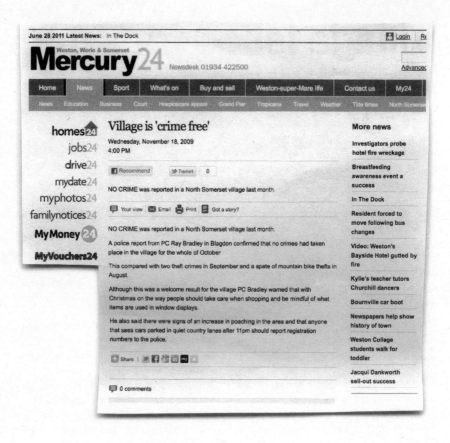

Village is 'crime free'

NO CRIME WAS reported in a North Somerset village last month.

A police report from PC Ray Bradley in Blagdon confirmed that no crimes had taken place in the village for the whole of October.

This compared with two theft crimes in September and a spate of mountain bike thefts in August.

Although this was a welcome result for the village PC Bradley warned that with Christmas on the way people should take care when shopping and be mindful of what items are used in window displays.

He also said there were signs of an increase in poaching in the area and that anyone who sees cars parked in quiet country lanes after 11pm should report registration numbers to the police.

Pensioner in pants foils angry burglar

Report by **CHARLOTTE RICHARDSON**
charlotte.richardson@archant.co.uk

A PLUCKY pensioner flew into action when he ran into the street in his underwear to fight off a violent burglar with an umbrella.

Ken Creffield says he 'felt like D'Artagnan' when he confronted intruder Daniel Jefferies and dodged flying lumps of concrete at his Thornbury Road home in Uphill.

The 75-year-old grandfather-of-five suffered bleeding next to his brain after the burglar attacked him, also hitting him over the head with a walking stick and an umbrella.

But Mr Creffield refused to let the 24-year-old criminal get away and held

him off with a golf umbrella in the street at 3.30am.

Jefferies, of no fixed abode, was jailed for two-and-a-half years at Bristol Crown Court last week as a result of the offence in July.

Mr Creffield said: "I woke up to shouting and banging in the street, but I was too sleepy to drag myself out of bed.

"But then I thought I heard a noise inside my house.

"I opened the door and there was a young guy on the landing.

"He pushed me in the throat and as I staggered back he whacked me on the head with a heavy ebony walking stick he had taken from my hall after kicking my front door in.

"I fell backwards but was instantly on my feet thanks to a surge of adrenaline."

Mr Creffield chased Jefferies down the stairs, but the intruder had grabbed a golf umbrella from the hall and hit the pensioner over the head with it.

Not wanting the burglar to get away, the grandfather, dressed in his underpants and a T-shirt, chased him into the street.

The former journalist added: "He tried to hit me a third time but I caught the umbrella as it came down and wrenched it from him.

"I decided to go after him

and after 100 yards he reappeared from a side street armed with two lumps of broken concrete.

"He threw the small lump at me and it hit my leg. I was holding the umbrella like D'Artagnan and Jefferies was holding the big concrete block like a club, ready to crash it down on my head or bare feet."

Mr Creffield ran home and called the police, who soon arrived, along with an ambulance that took the pensioner to hospital.

A day later he was diagnosed with bleeding next to the brain, known as a subdural haematoma.

Mr Creffield said: "This is a killer condition and one in five people suffering with it dies.

"I am on the mend now, but my memory and energy levels are affected.

"I have no vengeful feelings towards Jefferies but I am glad he is in jail.

"He needs to be locked away until he ceases to be a danger to the public."

Jefferies, who was 23 years old at the time of the offence, previously pleaded guilty to the burglary.

Pictured: Ken Creffield.

Pensioner in pants foils angry burglar

By Charlotte Richardson

A PLUCKY PENSIONER flew into action when he ran into the street in his underwear to fight off a violent burglar with an umbrella.

Ken Creffield says he 'felt like D'Artagnan' when he confronted intruder Daniel Jefferies and dodged flying lumps of concrete at his Thornbury Road home in Uphill.

The 75-year-old grandfather of five suffered bleeding next to his brain after the burglar attacked him, also hitting him over the head with a walking stick and an umbrella.

But Mr Creffield refused to let the 24-year-old criminal get away and held him off with a golf umbrella in the street at 3.30am.

Jefferies, of no fixed abode, was jailed for two and a half years at Bristol Crown Court last week as a result of the offence in July.

Mr Creffield said: 'I woke up to shouting and banging in the street, but I was too sleepy to drag myself out of bed.

'But then I thought I heard a noise inside my house.

'I opened the door and there was a young guy on the landing.

'He pushed me in the throat and as I staggered back he whacked me on the head with a heavy ebony walking stick he had taken from my hall after kicking my front door in.

'I fell backwards but was instantly on my feet thanks to a surge of adrenaline.'

Mr Creffield chased Jefferies down the stairs, but the intruder had grabbed a golf umbrella from the hall and hit the pensioner over the head with it.

Not wanting the burglar to get away, the grandfather, dressed in his underpants and a T-shirt, chased him into the street.

The former journalist added: 'He tried to hit me a third time but I caught the umbrella as it came down and wrenched it from him.

'I decided to go after him and after 100 yards he reappeared from a side street armed with two lumps of broken concrete.

'He threw the small lump at me and it hit my leg. I was holding the umbrella like D'Artagnan and Jefferies was holding the big concrete block like a club, ready to crash it down on my head or bare feet.'

Mr Creffield ran home and called the police, who soon arrived, along with an ambulance that took the pensioner to hospital.

Jefferies, who was 23 years old at the time of the offence, previously pleaded guilty to the burglary.

27

Archived Headlines
December 24-30, 2007

No evidence of drink-driving detected

More than 80 vehicles were stopped over the course of last weekend during the festive road safety campaign.
Sergeant Gordon Deans said police were "extremely pleased" to report that no evidence of drink-driving was found. He said there were a few minor defects detected.
"It is hoped that this trend will continue over the festive period and beyond," he added.

Negative breath tests in road safety campaign

Over the weekend, 18 negative breath tests were provided by motorists in Orkney, as part of the festive road safety campaign.
One positive roadside breath test was provided, but after further investigation, the driver was found to be just under the 35 microgram limit.

No evidence of drink-driving detected

MORE THAN 80 vehicles were stopped over the course of last weekend during the festive road safety campaign.

Sergeant Gordon Deans said police were 'extremely pleased' to report that no evidence of drink-driving was found. He said there were a few minor defects detected.

Negative breath tests in road safety campaign

OVER THE WEEKEND, 18 negative breath tests were provided by motorists in Orkney, as part of the festive road safety campaign.

One positive roadside breath test was provided, but after further investigation, the driver was found to be just under the 35 microgram limit.

No charges for man, 37

A MAN arrested on suspicion of assaulting a female traffic warden on Carlisle's busiest shopping street has been released without charge.

Prosecutors have decided to take no further action against the 37-year-old after he was held following an allegation he attacked a parking attendant.

The man was due to answer bail after being arrested last month.

But a force spokeswoman said: "After consultation with the Crown Prosecution Service there is to be no further action on this case."

Police confirmed they are not looking for anybody else in connection with the incident.

The man had been arrested following allegations a traffic warden had been assaulted as she ticketed a motorcycle on English Street on Friday, August 15 at 4pm.

The Crown Prosecution Service decides if prosecutions should be pursued.

No charges for man, 37

A MAN ARRESTED on suspicion of assaulting a female traffic warden on Carlisle's busiest shopping street has been released without charge.

Prosecutors have decided to take no further action against the 37-year-old after he was held following an allegation he attacked a parking attendant.

The man was due to answer bail after being arrested last month.

But a force spokeswoman said: 'After consultation with the Crown Prosecution Service there is to be no further action on this case.'

Police confirmed they are not looking for anybody else in connection with the incident.

The man had been arrested following allegations a traffic warden had been assaulted as she ticketed a motorcycle on English Street on Friday, August 15 at 4pm.

The Crown Prosecution Service decides if prosecutions should be pursued.

Paul Goulding with one of his hanging baskets. A basket planted by his partner's children was stolen on Sunday but returned on Monday evening. Picture: Terry Habgood.

Mystery as hanging basket is stolen – then returned

A COUPLE in Onslow Village is no closer to solving the mystery of why a hanging basket was snatched from their doorstep, only to be returned two days later.

The basket, which was overflowing with white and purple flowers, was stolen on Sunday while owners Nicole Van Staven and her partner, Paul Goulding, were out.

However, the thieves seemed to have suffered an attack of conscience when it was returned, and placed next to her car, with only a few snapped stems.

Miss Van Staven said it meant they would no longer show off their colourful displays. It had been planted from scratch by her children two months ago and was put alongside her two other baskets, which were left untouched.

"I had three hanging baskets and they went for that one," she said. "It was put up in a way that people could come up the road and have a look at it. It's got to the stage now where you

are scared to put things outside your own home."

However, the couple did not think it would be worth contacting the police about the theft, despite the effort that had gone into it.

"We were just as stunned to find it returned as we were when it was stolen," Miss Van Staven said, "I wasn't looking for it or anything. Maybe somebody overheard me talking about it or something.

"No question, we are going to put them under padlock and

key at the back now."

Mr Goulding said he believed their property had been targeted but hoped other people would not be put off decorating the outside of their homes.

"It's more annoying that you actually make the effort to put flowers up and make the house look good," he said. "We paid about £30 to £40 to put it together. It's a shame because Guildford is a nice town, but not when things like this happen."

Mystery as hanging basket is stolen – then returned

A COUPLE IN Onslow Village is no closer to solving the mystery of why a hanging basket was snatched from their doorstep, only to be returned two days later.

The basket, which was overflowing with white and purple flowers, was stolen on Sunday while owners Nicole Van Staven and her partner, Paul Goulding, were out.

However, the thieves seemed to have suffered an attack of conscience when it was returned, and placed next to her car, with only a few snapped stems.

Miss Van Staven said it meant they would no longer show off their colourful displays. It had been planted from scratch by her children two months ago and was put alongside her two other baskets, which were left untouched.

'I had three hanging baskets and they went for that one,' she said. 'It was put up in a way that people could come up the road and have a look at it. It's got to the stage now where you are scared to put things outside your own home.'

However, the couple did not think it would be worth contacting the police about the theft, despite the effort that had gone into it.

'We were just as stunned to find it returned as we were when it was stolen,' Miss Van Staven said. 'I wasn't looking for it or anything. Maybe somebody overheard me talking about it or something.

'No question, we are going to put them under padlock and key at the back now.'

Mr Goulding said he believed their property had been targeted but hoped other people would not be put off decorating the outside of their homes.

'It's more annoying that you actually make the effort to put flowers up and make the house look good,' he said. 'We paid about £30 to £40 to put it together. It's a shame because Guildford is a nice town, but not when things like this happen.'

Milk stolen from outside property

MILK was stolen from outside a house in Old Shoreham Road, Southwick, just after 1am on Friday.

Two people were seen getting into a blue hatchback car.

Milk stolen from outside property

MILK WAS STOLEN from outside a house in Old Shoreham Road, Southwick, just after 1am on Friday.

Two people were seen getting into a blue hatchback car.

this is ▶ Login ▶ Register

Lincolnshire

I'm looking for   e.g. pubs   ⊙ Our site

News Sport Forums What's On **Deals** **Pictures** **Jobs** **Motors** **Homes** R

Arrest made in pie theft mystery

this is **This is Lincolnshire** ▶ Follow   Monday, February 15, 2010

A TEENAGER has been arrested after hundreds of pies were stolen from a Boston butchers.

Around £400 worth of pies and cooked meats were stolen when the shop in the Market Place was broken into on February 8.

Pie

A 19-year-old man has been arrested on suspicion of burglary and released on bail to return to Spalding Police Station on Saturday.

👍 0 recommendations   ▶ Tweet   f Share   ◀ Share   ▶ Report

Arrest made in pie theft mystery

By G. Holmes

A TEENAGER HAS been arrested after hundreds of pies were stolen from a Boston butchers.

Around £400 worth of pies and cooked meats were stolen when the shop in the Market Place was broken into on February 8.

A 19-year-old man has been arrested on suspicion of burglary and released on bail to return to Spalding Police Station on Saturday.

The Argus

News | Sport | Albion | The Guide | Magazine | Photos | Fan

Business News | Council Election Results 2011 | Comment | Le

The Argus » News »

NEWS 🔊 ⊹ SEND YOUR NEWS, PICTURES & VIDEO

Hunt for Worthing "poo thief"

12:45pm Wednesday 10th March 2010

By Ben Parsons, Crime Reporter »

🖶 Print ✉ Email 💬 Comments(26)

🐦 Tweet 0 📘 Recommend

A bag-snatcher on a bicycle pinched a bag of poo from an elderly dog-walker in Worthing.

The thief rode past the pensioner near the Post Office in High Street, Tarring, and grabbed a bag she had been using to clean up after her dog.

A spokeswoman for Sussex Police said: "A male on his pushbike came past her and snatched the bag, perhaps thinking that there was something of value inside.

"The lady was not harmed and clearly the thief stole nothing of value."

The crime took place at 10.45am on Sunday.

The suspect was described as a black teenager.

Anyone with information is asked to call Sussex Police on 0845 6070999.

Hunt for Worthing 'poo thief'

By Ben Parsons

A BAG-SNATCHER ON a bicycle pinched a bag of poo from an elderly dog-walker in Worthing.

The thief rode past the pensioner near the Post Office in High Street, Tarring, and grabbed a bag she had been using to clean up after her dog.

A spokeswoman for Sussex Police said: 'A male on his pushbike came past her and snatched the bag, perhaps thinking that there was something of value inside.

'The lady was not harmed and clearly the thief stole nothing of value.'

The crime took place at 10.45am on Sunday.

The suspect was described as a black teenager.

Anyone with information is asked to call Sussex Police on 0845 6070999.

Evening

Voice of Calderdale

COURIER

37,817   Halifax, Wednesday, September 30, 1998

Cow attacks school cook

A SCHOOL cook has had to have emergency surgery after she and her dog were attacked by a cow while they walked in a field.

Mrs Charlotte Kyle, cook-in-charge at St John's Church of England Junior and Infant School, Rishworth, suffered serious injuries to her finger and her dog, Nikki, is still recovering at the vets after two operations.

Mrs Kyle, of Regal Drive, Rishworth, was walking her 15-year-old cross border collie through a field between Rishworth New Road and Shaw Lane, Rishworth.

She was using a public footpath and the dog was a few feet in front when the cow kicked it into the air.

Mrs Kyle's husband, Doug, said as she went to pick up the dog the cow lashed out again.

It is not clear if the cow bit Mrs Kyle or kicked her. "It all happened so quickly," he said.

His wife was taken to the Royal Halifax Infirmary but later transferred to the plastic surgery unit at Bradford Royal Infirmary.

Her finger was hanging off and doctors had to sew it back on. They do not know yet if the operation will be successful.

"My wife might still lose part of her finger - it's been smashed."

Mrs Kyle was very distressed after the incident and is unlikely to return to work for at least six weeks.

The dog is still recovering at Prospect Veterinary Centre, Sowerby Bridge.

The field is regularly used by people but Mr Kyle said there was no reason why the farmer should not put cows in it. "If you live in a semi-rural area these things can happen," he said.

The field is owned by Mr Kevin Horsfall, of Soyland. His wife today refused to comment.

Cow attacks school cook

A SCHOOL COOK has had to have emergency surgery after she and her dog were attacked by a cow while they walked in a field.

Mrs Charlotte Kyle, cook-in-charge at St John's Church of England Junior and Infant School, Rishworth, suffered serious injuries to her finger and her dog, Nikki, is still recovering at the vet's after two operations.

Mrs Kyle, of Regal Drive, Rishworth, was walking her 15-year-old cross border collie through a field between Rishworth New Road and Shaw Lane, Rishworth.

She was using a public footpath and the dog was a few feet in front when the cow kicked it into the air. Mrs Kyle's husband, Doug, said as she went to pick up the dog the cow lashed out again.

It is not clear if the cow bit Mrs Kyle or kicked her. 'It all happened so quickly,' he said.

His wife was taken to the Royal Halifax Infirmary but later transferred to the plastic surgery unit at Bradford Royal Infirmary.

Her finger was hanging off and doctors had to sew it back on. They do not know yet if the operation will be successful.

'My wife might still lose part of her finger – it's been smashed.'

Mrs Kyle was very distressed after the incident and is unlikely to return to work for at least six weeks.

The dog is still recovering at Prospect Veterinary Centre, Sowerby Bridge.

The field is regularly used by people but Mr Kyle said there was no reason why the farmer should not put cows in it. 'If you live in a semi-rural area these things can happen,' he said.

The field is owned by Mr Kevin Horsfall, of Soyland. His wife today refused to comment.

NEWSfile

Boiled egg explodes

AN ELDERLY woman exploded a boiled egg.

The teatime disaster happened at 4.44pm on Tuesday (July 22) in Newton House, Plas Newton Lane.

Crews from Chester fire station were called to the scene.

Watch manager Chris Roddaway, at Chester fire station, said: "She boiled it dry – they just go bang and it blackened the pan."

Boiled egg explodes

AN ELDERLY WOMAN exploded a boiled egg.

The teatime disaster happened at 4.44pm on Tuesday (July 22) in Newton House, Plas Newton Lane.

Crews from Chester fire station were called to the scene.

Watch manager Chris Roddaway, at Chester fire station, said: 'She boiled it dry – they just go bang and it blackened the pan.'

Horsham coat hanger theft – verdict

Surrey police report no deaths in custody

Police called to pull up drunk's knickers

COWS ON THE RUN AFTER TRACTOR THEFT

Chocolate cake scandal hits Skye festival

Man died of natural causes

Nature

Guilty: Michael Robert Pierce shot badger dead with rifle

CSI-style tests reveal locksmith killed badger

By PHIL GOODWIN
pgoodwin@c-dm.co.uk

A ST Ives locksmith was convicted of killing a badger after a forensic weapons expert matched his rifle to a bullet found in the animal.

Michael Robert Pierce, of Love Lane, denied wilfully shooting the protected animal, at Penderleath caravan park at Towednack last year, saying a chronic back problem had kept him from hunting.

After two days of detailed and conflicting ballistics evidence from two scientific experts, magistrates at Truro ruled that his CZ .22-calibre rifle had fired the fatal shot.

The 57-year-old faced two charges under the 1992 Protection of Badgers Act: that he unlawfully killed the animal and used a firearm and ammunition insufficiently powerful to do so humanely.

Fined

He was fined £300, ordered to pay £1,930 in costs and forfeited his rifle and gun licence on Tuesday.

Julian Herbert, prosecuting, said after the trial that he believed the sentence would "send out a message that this sort of behaviour towards badgers will not be tolerated".

Early in the morning of September 23, park co-owner Christopher Maskell found the dying badger while walking his dog near the Cornish hedge

■ Sergeant Simon Dobson. 0911JJ00403badger

bordering Chy and Bal Farm.

Police wildlife officer, Simon Dobson, took the corpse to a government laboratory in Truro for a post-mortem examination the following day.

Veterinary investigation officer, Adrian Colloff, found a bullet lodged in the abdomen, which was later identified as a .22 calibre round.

Sgt Dobson then scoured the database of gun licences for local shooters with permission to hunt in the area and who owned similar rifles.

Pierce, a firearms licence holder, had written consent to shoot rabbits on the 80-acre estate from farm owner Mary Osborne, and had hunted there for 10 years.

In March, Sgt Dobson seized a CZ rifle from Pierce's home,

later using it to fire test rounds at Helston Gunsmiths, which were subsequently analysed by ballistic experts.

Pierce, a diabetic who never hunted alone, said his arrest in April had been like a bolt from the blue.

Describing himself as a "good citizen" who subscribed to Greenpeace, he claimed he "enjoyed wildlife immensely" - only hunting for food and never for sport.

He said that at the time of the offence he had been on crutches and effectively unable to walk, let alone carry guns, lamps and bags over rugged ground.

"I have never, ever killed or knowingly aimed at a badger," he said. "If I want to shoot for recreation I use targets or clay pigeons."

"My job is a position of trust and I would not do anything to jeopardise that or my shooting certificate."

Defending, Charles Hart, said there were four or five people shooting the land but the investigation trail had gone dead once the incriminating ballistic report arrived.

Complex case

"From then on, Sergeant Dobson was paying lip service to the investigation because he thought he had got his man," he said.

Sgt Dobson said it had been a "complex and involved case" and he had acted on evidence showing a perfect conclusive match.

"Badgers are protected by law and cases like this are a positive way to demonstrate this to the public," he said.

Robert Speechley, of Cornwall Badger Rescue, who attended the trial, said he hoped the ruling "would make people think twice before shooting protected species".

"We believe there are many badgers being killed in illegal ways, but we rarely find them and it is unusual to see a case with such good evidence as this one."

■ Michael Pierce leaving the court. 0911JJ00401badger

■ The badger shot by Pierce.

■ Michael Pierce's gun. 0911JJ00402badger

Experts failed to agree on fire test results

A SINGLE rifle shot fired across Penwith farmland led to a courtroom tussle between leading forensic experts, worthy of the TV series Crime Scene Investigations.

Following a year-long police operation, evidence gleaned from the macroscopic analysis of two rifles and a clutch of bullets was finally presented to magistrates.

Prosecution expert Philip Boyce, of Key Forensics - a commended senior scientist in Northern Ireland during the Troubles - was commissioned to match the question bullet from the dead badger to those

fired by a weapon seized by police.

Mr Boyce, a veteran of investigations in Iraq and Afghanistan, scrutinised the six right-hand twists imprinted on the blood and tissue-stained .22 subsonic bullet from the badger, referred to as exhibit SAD9.

After painstaking analysis, he declared it to bear almost identical markings to the five hollow point bullets, test fired from Mr Pierce's gun into a cotton-wool-filled catching box at Helston Gunsmiths.

He said there was sufficient evidence to conclude that the

■ The bullet.

animal could only have been killed by the Pierce rifle, or SAD 10.

The defence suggested police analyse the .22 weapon of another known local shooter and

licence holder. An identical model of the CZ, owned by William Richard Rowe, was sent to Mr Boyce's Key Forensics lab in Warrington for comparison, exhibit SAD25.

This weapon was ruled out by Mr Boyce after test firings did not match bullet SAD9.

The defence drafted in a second firearms expert, former South African policeman Andre Horne, from LGC Forensics in Leeds, his first court appearance for the defence in 14 years.

Mr Horne, an FBI-trained practitioner, cast doubt on the findings and refused to rule in

or out either Pierce's or Rowe's gun.

Mr Horne said: "I could not possibly call it a positive identification - the big markings were nowhere to be seen on the question bullet so I had to call it as inconclusive."

He revealed that it was extremely rare for himself and Mr Boyce to disagree, which he felt was significant enough to cast reasonable doubt.

But after deliberation the magistrates opted to side with the first report by Mr Boyce and ruled that it had been the Pierce rifle which had fired the shot.

Badger shot by St Ives Locksmith

CSI-style tests reveal locksmith killed badger

Guilty: Michael Robert Pierce shot badger dead with rifle

By Phil Goodwin

A ST IVES locksmith was convicted of killing a badger after a forensic weapons expert matched his rifle to a bullet found in the animal.

Michael Robert Pierce, of Love Lane, denied wilfully shooting the protected animal, at Penderleath caravan park at Towednack last year, saying a chronic back problem had kept him from hunting.

After two days of detailed and conflicting ballistics evidence from two scientific experts, magistrates at Truro ruled that his CZ .22-calibre rifle had fired the fatal shot.

The 57-year-old faced two charges under the 1992 Protection of Badgers Act: that he unlawfully killed the animal and used a firearm and ammunition insufficiently powerful to do so humanely.

Fined

He was fined £300, ordered to pay £1,930 in costs and forfeited his rifle and gun licence on Tuesday.

Julian Herbert, prosecuting, said after the trial that he believed the sentence would 'send out a message that this sort of behaviour towards badgers will not be tolerated'.

Early in the morning of September 23, park co-owner Christopher Maskell found the dying badger while walking his dog near the Cornish hedge bordering Chy and Bal Farm.

Police wildlife officer, Simon Dobson, took the corpse to a government laboratory in Truro for a post-mortem examination the following day.

Veterinary investigation officer, Adrian Colloff, found a bullet lodged in the abdomen, which was later identified as a .22 calibre round.

Sgt Dobson then scoured the database of gun licences for local shooters with permission to hunt in the area and who owned similar rifles.

Pierce, a firearms licence holder, had written consent to shoot rabbits on the 80-acre estate from farm owner Mary

cont. on page 54

Osborne, and had hunted there for 10 years.

In March, Sgt Dobson seized a CZ rifle from Pierce's home, later using it to fire test rounds at Helston Gunsmiths, which were subsequently analysed by ballistic experts.

Pierce, a diabetic who never hunted alone, said his arrest in April had been like a bolt from the blue.

Describing himself as a 'good citizen' who subscribed to Greenpeace, he claimed he 'enjoyed wildlife immensely' – only hunting for food and never for sport.

He said that at the time of the offence he had been on crutches and effectively unable to walk, let alone carry guns, lamps and bags over rugged ground.

'I have never, ever killed or knowingly aimed at a badger,' he said. 'If I want to shoot for recreation I use targets or clay pigeons.

'My job is a position of trust and I would not do anything to jeopardise that or my shooting certificate.'

Defending, Charles Hart, said there were four or five people shooting the land but the investigation trail had gone dead once the incriminating ballistic report arrived.

Complex case

'From then on, Sergeant Dobson was paying lip service to the investigation because he thought he had got his man,' he said.

Sgt Dobson said it had been a 'complex and involved case' and he had acted on evidence showing a perfect conclusive match.

'Badgers are protected by law and cases like this are a positive way to demonstrate this to the public,' he said.

Robert Speechley, of Cornwall Badger Rescue, who attended the trial, said he hoped the ruling 'would make people think twice before shooting protected species'.

'We believe there are many badgers being killed in illegal ways, but we rarely find them and it is unusual to see a case with such good evidence as this one.'

Experts failed to agree on fire test results

A SINGLE RIFLE shot fired across Penwith farmland led to a courtroom tussle between leading forensic experts, worthy of the TV series *Crime Scene Investigations*.

Following a year-long police operation, evidence gleaned from the microscopic analysis of two rifles and a clutch of bullets was finally presented to magistrates.

Prosecution expert Philip Boyce, of Key Forensics – a commended senior scientist in Northern Ireland during the Troubles – was commissioned to match the question bullet from the dead badger to those fired by a weapon seized by police.

Mr Boyce, a veteran of investigations in Iraq and Afghanistan, scrutinised the six right-hand twists imprinted on the blood and tissue-stained .22 subsonic bullet from the badger, referred to as exhibit SAD9.

After painstaking analysis, he declared it to bear almost identical markings to the five hollow point bullets, test fired from Mr Pierce's gun into a cotton-wool-filled catching box at Helston Gunsmiths.

He said there was sufficient evidence to conclude that the animal could only have been killed by the Pierce rifle, or SAD10.

The defence suggested police analyse the .22 weapon of another known local shooter and licence holder. An identical model of the CZ, owned by William Richard Rowe, was sent to Mr Boyce's Key Forensics lab in Warrington for comparison, exhibit SAD25.

This weapon was ruled out by Mr Boyce after test firings did not match bullet SAD9.

The defence drafted in a second firearms expert, former South African policeman Andre Horne, from LGC Forensics in Leeds, his first court appearance for the defence in 14 years.

Mr Horne, an FBI-trained practitioner, cast doubt on the findings and refused to rule in or out either Pierce's or Rowe's gun.

Mr Horne said: 'I could not possibly call it a positive identification – the big markings were nowhere to be seen on the question bullet so I had to call it as inconclusive.'

He revealed that it was extremely rare for himself and Mr Boyce to disagree, which he felt was significant enough to cast reasonable doubt.

But after deliberation the magistrates opted to side with the first report by Mr Boyce and ruled that it had been the Pierce rifle which had fired the shot.

Man, 39, faces charges of allowing donkey to attack others

Animals 'terrorised by bossy donkey'

By John Harrison
Chronicle Reporter
john.harrison@northantsnews.co.uk

A MAN has appeared in court charged with failing to prevent a "violent and bossy" donkey from terrorising a field of farm animals.

Andrew Harding, aged 39, appeared before Daventry Magistrates' Court yesterday to face eight charges of animal neglect and allowing a vicious Spanish donkey to attack rare breed pigs, pygmy goats and other donkeys.

Prosecuting on behalf of Northamptonshire County Council, Vic Smith told the court that Mr Harding rented a field off High Street, in Tiffield, near Towcester.

The court heard Harding had taken a male show donkey, named Paco, on a trial basis from Karen Beare, the manager of the field.

Harding had taken temporary ownership of the donkey in December 2008, as a Christmas present for his children and with the intention of buying him at a later date.

Giving evidence, Mrs Beare told the court she had given Harding the donkey on the condition he was kept away from his pigs, goats and sheep as Paco was "bossy" and could potentially hurt them. However, by March the following year, residents reported seeing Paco attacking the animals on a daily basis.

The court was shown a DVD of Paco chasing a black Kune Kune pig, cornering it, grabbing it with his teeth and shaking it.

Giving evidence, Paul Flowers, who rented a neighbouring field, told magistrates he believed Paco had also killed one of his donkeys, named Pedro.

Mr Flowers said: "I saw the pigs had bite marks on their necks. I saw one of the goats grabbed by the neck and thrown against a shed. On another day I had to fight Paco to get him off a pig.

"About two days later I found one of my donkeys dead in the field."

Pablo, who was bought for Mr Flowers' daughter who has special educational needs, was found with bite marks on his neck and signs that he had been trampled.

Trading standards officers contacted Harding several times to ask him to make sure Paco was kept separately from the rest of his animals. However, they say he failed to put up fences capable of keeping the animals apart.

Harding, of Bretby Chase, Westcroft, in Milton Keynes, denies six counts of breaking the Animal Welfare Act 2006 and two charges of breaching farming regulations.

The case continues.

Animals 'terrorised by bossy donkey'

By John Harrison

A MAN HAS appeared in court charged with failing to prevent a 'violent and bossy' donkey from terrorising a field of farm animals.

Andrew Harding, aged 39, appeared before Daventry Magistrates' Court yesterday to face eight charges of animal neglect and allowing a vicious Spanish donkey to attack rare breed pigs, pygmy goats and other donkeys.

Prosecuting on behalf of Northamptonshire County Council, Vic Smith told the court that Mr Harding rented a field off High Street, in Tiffield, near Towcester.

The court heard Harding had taken a male show donkey, named Paco, on a trial basis from Karen Beare, the manager of the field.

Harding had taken temporary ownership of the donkey in December 2008, as a Christmas present for his children and with the intention of buying him at a later date.

Giving evidence, Mrs Beare told the court she had given Harding the donkey on the condition he was kept away from his pigs, goats and sheep as Paco was 'bossy' and could potentially hurt them. However, by March the following year, residents reported seeing Paco attacking the animals on a daily basis.

The court was shown a DVD of Paco chasing a black Kune Kune pig, cornering it, grabbing it with his teeth and shaking it.

Giving evidence, Paul Flowers, who rented a neighbouring field, told magistrates he believed Paco had also killed one of his donkeys, named Pedro.

Mr Flowers said: 'I saw the pigs had bite marks on their necks. I saw one of the goats grabbed by the neck and thrown against a shed. On another day I had to fight Paco to get him off a pig.

'About two days later I found one of my donkeys dead in the field.'

Pedro, who was bought for Mr Flowers' daughter who has special educational needs, was found with bite marks on his neck and signs that he had been trampled.

Trading standards officers contacted Harding several times to ask him to make sure Paco was kept separately from the rest of his animals. However, they say he failed to put up fences capable of keeping the animals apart.

Harding, of Bretby Chase, Westcroft, in Milton Keynes, denies six counts of breaking the Animal Welfare Act 2006 and two charges of breaching farming regulations.

The case continues.

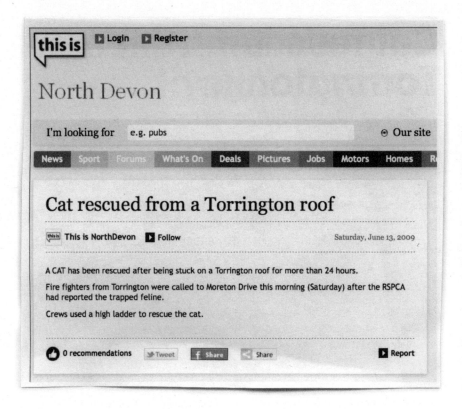

Cat rescued from a Torrington roof

By L. Churchill

A CAT HAS been rescued after being stuck on a Torrington roof for more than 24 hours.

Firefighters from Torrington were called to Moreton Drive this morning (Saturday) after the RSPCA had reported the trapped feline.

Crews used a high ladder to rescue the cat.

Chicken in a basque shock for cop

A MAN caught with a prostitute gave police an unwelcome surprise.

He was wearing a woman's lacy basque containing chicken fillets.

Peter Jackson, aged 52, of Entwisle Road, Heybrook, was spotted with a prostitute in Kenion Street last November, Rochdale Magistrates were told.

Yvonne Tunicliffe, prosecuting, said two plain clothes policemen, who were patrolling the area, followed the pair to a quiet corner of a car park.

When they approached Jackson he said: "Do you mind if I get changed first?" Miss Tunicliffe said he had been wearing a shirt and underneath he wore a basque, containing 'what appeared to be uncooked chicken fillets' in the brassiere cups.

Asked why he was wearing the bizarre outfit, he replied: "I like wearing them, it's just my thing."

The court heard that Jackson had previously served a custodial sentence for an indecent act on a child.

He admitted a charge of soliciting a woman for the purpose of prostitution and was fined £50 with £35 court costs.

Chicken in a basque shock for cop

A MAN CAUGHT with a prostitute gave police an unwelcome surprise. He was wearing a woman's lacy basque containing chicken fillets.

Peter Jackson, aged 52, of Entwisle Road, Heybrook, was spotted with a prostitute in Kenion Street last November, Rochdale Magistrates were told.

Yvonne Tunicliffe, prosecuting, said two plain clothes policemen, who were patrolling the area, followed the pair to a quiet corner of a car park.

When they approached Jackson, he said: 'Do you mind if I get changed first?'

Miss Tunicliffe said he had been wearing a shirt and underneath he wore a basque, containing 'what appeared to be uncooked chicken fillets' in the brassiere cups.

Asked why he was wearing the bizarre outfit, he replied: 'I like wearing them, it's just my thing.'

The court heard that Jackson had previously served a custodial sentence for an indecent act on a child.

He admitted a charge of soliciting a woman for the purpose of prostitution and was fined £50 with £35 court costs.

Curious cat is rescued from tin

FIRE fighters were called to Torrington to free a curious cat that got its head stuck in a tin can.

The cat was also trapped on the roof of a building in Mill Street on Sunday lunchtime.

The fire crew from Torrington used a ladder to rescue the cat from the rooftop.

Curious cat is rescued from tin

FIREFIGHTERS WERE CALLED to Torrington to free a curious cat that got its head stuck in a tin can.

The cat was also trapped on the roof of a building in Mill Street on Sunday lunch-time.

The fire crew from Torrington used a ladder to rescue the cat from the rooftop.

Dog injures nose

By Karen Bate

POLICE IN RINGWOOD are investigating the circumstances surrounding an injury to a dog's nose.

A woman was walking her dog and puppy, when her puppy ran off.

Her dog ran after the puppy but collided with a male dog walker and his dog.

The woman's dog received an injury to his nose.

THE COURIER

News   **Sport**   **Lifestyle**   **Community**

Sunday 12 June 2011   Log in   Register

You are here News > Local > Features

Don't let your dog eat anti-freeze, says Whitnash vet

Published on **Tuesday 16 December 2008 09:31**

We are having some lovely crisp cold winter days at the moment. The frosted leaves and delicate fern-like patterns of the ice are beautiful.

However all this wintery weather does bring it's problems and our pets are not immune from these.

The cold weather tends to make aches and pains worse so arthritic cats and dogs can suffer more during the winter months.

It is important to make sure they have access to warm, well padded beds and if they get cold or wet when outside, then dry and warm them once back in the house.

Arthritic dogs cope much better with frequent short walks during the day rather than one long one- this keeps them supple without putting too much strain on aching legs and also keeps muscles strong which help support the joints.

There are lots of different treatment options for arthritis in animals so if your pet is a bit stiff then it would be worth discussing the options with your vet.

Another risk during cold weather is antifreeze poisoning. Fortunately it is not common as most animals do not get access to it but we have seen several suspected cases of it recently.

Antifreeze has a sweet taste and unfortunately some animals find it attractive.

Don't let your dog eat antifreeze, says Whitnash vet

WE ARE HAVING some lovely crisp cold winter days at the moment. The frosted leaves and delicate fern-like patterns of the ice are beautiful.

However, all this wintery weather does bring its problems and our pets are not immune from these.

The cold weather tends to make aches and pains worse so arthritic cats and dogs can suffer more during the winter months.

It is important to make sure they have access to warm, well-padded beds and if they get cold or wet when outside, then dry and warm them once back in the house.

Arthritic dogs cope much better with frequent short walks during the day rather than one long one – this keeps them supple without putting too much strain on aching legs and also keeps muscles strong which help support the joints.

There are lots of different treatment options for arthritis in animals, so if your pet is a bit stiff then it would be worth discussing the options with your vet.

Another risk during cold weather is antifreeze poisoning. Fortunately it is not common as most animals do not get access to it but we have seen several suspected cases of it recently.

Antifreeze has a sweet taste and unfortunately some animals find it attractive.

By the time the animal shows signs of problems, it is almost always too late to save them, causing, amongst other things, rapid kidney failure.

So if you are using antifreeze at home, please make sure the container is well hidden from any pets and make sure any spillages etc. are cleaned up before any animals can get to them.

Emily Emerson is a vet at Heathcote Veterinary Centre, Whitnash.

Sunday, 12 June 2011

Wilts and Gloucestershire
Standard

News | Sport | Leisure | Photosales | Info | Your Say | Events | Reader's Letters |

Royal Wedding celebrations | North Wilts news | Picture Gallery | National News | Features | Court Nev

Wilts and Gloucestershire Standard » News »

NEWS 🔊

Firefighters called to Standard offices to rescue a pigeon

1:41pm Friday 10th July 2009

🖨 Print | ✉ Email | 🔄 Share | 💬 Comments(1)

By Andy Woolfoot »

THE firefighters currently climbing a ladder outside of our Dyer Street office are rescuing a pigeon.

A pigeon became entangled in the anti-pigeon netting at some point before our staff arrived at work this morning.

After consultation with the Oak and Furrows Wildlife Rescue Centre in Somerford Keynes and the RSCPA it became necessary to involve the fire service.

We apologise to anyone inconvenienced by the road closure and we will bring you an update of the status of the pigeon later this afternoon.

Firefighters called to *Standard* offices to rescue a pigeon

THE FIREFIGHTERS CURRENTLY climbing a ladder outside of our Dyer Street office are rescuing a pigeon.

A pigeon became entangled in the anti-pigeon netting at some point before our staff arrived at work this morning.

After consultation with the Oak and Furrows Wildlife Rescue Centre in Somerford Keynes and the RSPCA it became necessary to involve the fire service.

We apologise to anyone inconvenienced by the road closure and we will bring you an update of the status of the pigeon later this afternoon.

Goldfish catch sparks debate

The capture of a 7lb 5oz goldfish from the UEA lake has sparked an interesting debate concering the original source of this surprise catch by Lowestoft angler Stuart Thurston and believed to be a national record even though goldfish are not listed by the British Rod-Caught Record Fish Committee.

The question that may remain unanswered is this: Was this fish originally one of the small Chinese goldfish that children used to win at village fairground coconut shies that had grown too big for its domestic environment, or was it a hybrid from the genes of an ornamental koi carp or a golden orfe (record 7lb 14oz) or a brown goldfish (5lb 11oz)?

Goldfish have turned up from time to time in local lakes and less frequently in local rivers and Broads where their vivid pigment always attracts the attention of a lurking pike that does not discriminate between the common and rare fish it regards as food.

More orange than gold: Stuart Thurston with his monster catch.

Goldfish catch sparks debate

THE CAPTURE OF a 7lb 5oz goldfish from the UEA lake has sparked an interesting debate concerning the original source of this surprise catch by Lowestoft angler Stuart Thurston and believed to be a national record even though goldfish are not listed by the British Rod-Caught Record Fish Committee.

The question that may remain un-answered is this: Was this fish originally one of the small Chinese goldfish that children used to win at village fairground coconut shies that had grown too big for its domestic environment, or was it a hybrid from the genes of an ornamental koi carp or a golden orfe (record 7lb 14oz) or a brown goldfish (5lb 11oz)?

Goldfish have turned up from time to time in local lakes and less frequently in local rivers and Broads where their vivid pigment always attracts the attention of a lurking pike that does not discriminate between the common and rare fish it regards as food.

LATE FINAL

The Gazette

THURSDAY, SEPTEMBER 5, 2002   No. 22,986   **NORTH WEST NEWSPAPER OF THE YEAR**

POLICE CALLED AFTER REV-UP RODENT GOES DRAG CAR RACING ON SEAFRONT

HAMSTER CAUGHT SPEEDING ON PROM

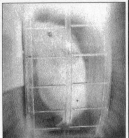

SPEED MERCHANT: Fast mover Speedy inside his hot rod wheel
Pictures: ROB LOCK

FAST ACTION: Six-year-old Chloe McArthur with Speedy in his wheels caught after hurtling down Cleveleys promenade like a rodent Michael Schumacher. Chloe is the granddaughter of the owners of Charnwood Kennels, Marton, where Speedy has been parked

By BEN BORLAND

A HOT rod hamster caused a stir when he was caught racing along the promenade – in his dragster car.

The renegade rodent sent day-trippers scurrying for cover with his high-speed antics on the seafront at Cleveleys.

But like all dangerous drivers, he was soon in the hands of the law and is now cooling off at a Fylde animal sanctuary where he has been nick-named Speedy.

PC Quentin Allen said there was amazement when the flying furball was handed in at Cleveleys police station.

The police log records: "A member of the public has handed in a hamster in a hot rod racing car."

TO PAGE FIVE

Hamster caught speeding on prom

Police called after rev-up rodent goes drag car racing on seafront

A HOT ROD hamster caused a stir when he was caught racing along the promenade – in his dragster car.

The renegade rodent sent day trippers scurrying for cover with his high-speed antics on the seafront at Cleveleys.

But like all dangerous drivers, he was soon in the hands of the law and is now cooling off at a Fylde animal sanctuary where he has been nicknamed Speedy.

PC Quentin Allen said there was amazement when the flying furball was handed in at Cleveleys police station.

The police log records: 'A member of the public has handed in a hamster in a hot rod racing car.

PC Allen said: 'It was a proper toy racing car with a hamster wheel in the middle and as the hamster runs it operates the car.

'You can just imagine a nice, sunny day on Cleveleys Prom, eating your chips and then this thing goes whizzing past.'

He added: 'It was quite amusing in here because whenever we tried to put Speedy down on the front desk he kept whizzing off trying to escape.

'It is the strangest thing I've dealt with in Cleveleys.'

The bemused bobbies handed the hamster over to Wadsworth Veterinary Surgery, North Shore.

Speedy was then transferred to the Fylde branch of the RSPCA in Fleetwood, and then to the 'high-security' Charnwood House Boarding Kennels in Marton.

Fylde RSPCA secretary Margaret Bysterbosch said: 'I have never heard of anything like this in 40 years in the organisation.

'I have seen everything from snakes to seals to lion cubs, but never a hamster bowling along the promenade in a racing car!'

But she added: 'It might seem amusing but it would not have been for the poor little soul if he hadn't been picked up. People should supervise their pets more closely.'

Nancy Williams, from Charnwood House, gave Speedy his nickname when the hamster and his hot rod arrived with them on Monday.

She said: 'He is a good hamster, he just goes a bit mad when he is behind the wheel. The vets said he was absolutely worn out when he got in – he must have gone for miles.

'We think somebody must have been playing with him outside and they have forgotten about him and he has just taken off.'

ABERYSTWYTH

Cambrian News

Eich wythnosolyn gorau ■ Your biggest-selling weekly newspaper   Established 1860   Thursday 21 June 2007   60p

I didn't know guinea pigs could swim!

Pictured with the rescued tortoises are Siobhan Price and Jonathan Burton, who are on work experience at the Animalarium, and volunteer Jasmine Bird.
DPJ21J116

by Norman Williams
norman@cambrian-news.co.uk

GUINEA pigs and tortoises were among the animals which had to be rescued as torrential rain hit Borth Animalarium and the Aberystwyth area this week.

Parts of the Animalarium were left under 12 inches of water while in Aberystwyth, a public house had to be evacuated and two theatre performances were cancelled.

And the wheels of justice came to a temporary halt because of storms and a power-cut - in Birmingham.

Borth Animalarium proprietor Jean Mumbray and her staff rescued a number of animals from the petting barn at about lunchtime on Friday.

She said: "It was not just the heavy rain causing a problem, but water running down the mountain and into the zoo.

"The petting barn was soon under about 12 inches of water, and after rescuing a ferret they managed to save rabbits and guinea pigs in there.

"When they got to the barn, the guinea pigs were swimming around - I didn't even know they could swim!"

And wooden pallets were put into a porcupine's cage, allowing it to scramble to safety.

The popular tourist attraction was closed on Saturday because it was deep in mud. But staff had cleared the area by Sunday, and it was 'business as usual'.

Sadly, however, there was one casualty, as a bat died.

Jean said: "It did not drown - we suspect that perhaps it died from shock."

Aberystwyth firefighters were also kept busy in Borth, pumping floodwater out a number of properties in Cae Gwylan. And they also pumped water off the B4353 Borth to Ynyslas road, which had become flooded.

In Aberystwyth, a hearing at the magistrates court was disrupted - because of storms and a power-cut in Birmingham!

A case being heard via video-link with a Birmingham prison came to a halt when the prison suffered a power-cut. The hearing was eventually resumed when the jail's power supply was restored some four hours later.

Yr Hen Orsaf Wetherspoons public house in Aberystwyth was evacuated for a short period at about 7.30pm, when water came streaming through a ceiling.

And the nearby Somerfield car park was under four inches of water.

There was flooding in Ffordd Sulien, Llanbadarn Fawr, and swift action was taken at the Black Lion where it was all staff hands to the pump to remove flood water.

Aberystwyth firefighters pumped water out of a property in Alexandra Road, and also attended to a dangerous manhole cover when water came gushing out of it, near Siop y Pethe, Owain Glyndŵr Square.

And ironically, the downpour forced the cancellation of two evening performances of outdoor production *A Few Little Drops*, at Aberystwyth Arts Centre. Audiences would have been invited to explore a flood-wrecked house, constructed outside the venue, as performers explored the strange properties of water - and its awesome power!

I didn't know guinea pigs could swim!

By Norman Williams

GUINEA PIGS AND tortoises were among the animals which had to be rescued as torrential rain hit Borth Animalarium and the Aberystwyth area this week.

Parts of the Animalarium were left under 12 inches of water while in Aberystwyth, a public house had to be evacuated and two theatre performances were cancelled.

Borth Animalarium proprietor Jean Mumbray and her staff rescued a number of animals from the petting barn at about lunchtime on Friday.

She said: 'It was not just the heavy rain causing a problem, but water running down the mountain and into the zoo.

'The petting barn was soon under about 12 inches of water, and after rescuing a ferret they managed to save rabbits and guinea pigs in there.

'When they got to the barn, the guinea pigs were swimming around – I didn't even know they could swim!'

And wooden pallets were put into a porcupine's cage, allowing it to scramble to safety.

The popular tourist attraction was closed on Saturday because it was deep in mud. But staff had cleared the area by Sunday, and it was 'business as usual'.

Sadly, however, there was one casualty, as a bat died.

Jean said: 'It did not drown – we suspect that perhaps it died from shock.'

Yr Hen Orsaf Wetherspoons public house in Aberystwyth was evacuated for a short period at about 7.30pm, when water came streaming through a ceiling.

And the nearby Somerfield car park was under four inches of water

There was flooding in Ffordd Sulien, Llanbadarn Fawr, and swift action was taken at the Black Lion where it was all staff hands to the pump to remove flood-water.

Aberystwyth firefighters pumped water out of a property in Alexandra Road, and also attended to a dangerous man-hole cover when water came gushing out of it, near Siop y Pethe, Owain Glyndwr Square.

And ironically, the downpour forced the cancellation of two evening performances of outdoor production *A Few Little Drops*, at Aberystwyth Arts Centre. Audiences would have been invited to explore a flood-wrecked house, constructed outside the venue, as performers explored the strange properties of water – and its awesome power!

SEAGULL
FLEW OFF
WITH CAT

making **local** matter **more**   Established 1863

WHITSTABLE
TIMES

visit our website
www.thisiskent.co.uk

Seagull flew off with cat

By J. Nurden

A STUNNED GRANDMOTHER looked on as a seagull swooped on her garden and lifted a terrified cat four feet off the ground.

Marion Clements, of Green Lane, Whitstable, says she almost choked on her tea when the bird picked the frightened feline up with its BEAK and attempted to fly away.

The 64-year-old, who runs Marion Clements clothes shop in the town, ran into her garden to find the black-and-white cat shivering with fear.

She said: 'It just stood there scared out of its wits. I went up to it but it ran off.

'I couldn't believe what had just happened. I've never seen anything like it in all my life.

'The poor cat was just minding its own business when the seagull swooped and grabbed the back of its neck with its beak.

'The bird must have got about four feet high before he dropped it.

'I ran outside because I wanted to get my two cats inside. They're both 15 and probably would have died if it had happened to them.

'My husband Barry would have gone mad. He'd shoot me before he'd shoot the cats.'

Since the attack on Friday morning Marion has kept a close eye on treasured pets Abby and Nicky.

She said: 'They're terrified now. When they go out in the garden they walk around the edge and hide behind the plants.

'I've got a broom at the ready just in case they try it on again.'

Marion says she has had the seagulls nesting on her roof for the last two months.

She said: 'They're an absolute nightmare.

'The noise is horrific and it starts about 4am every day.

'It wasn't so bad at first but now they have babies and are really protective of them.

'I'm just worried that they'll attack again. I have my two grandchildren round every week and I won't let them sit in the garden just in case.

'I rang the council and they just said, "We don't do seagulls."

'I couldn't believe it. They say they need to protect the birds but who's going to protect us?

'I've half a mind to go out in the garden with an air gun. That would soon sort them out.'

City council spokesman Rob Davies said: 'The council does not offer a service for the removal of seagulls.

'Anyone experiencing problems should contact a private pest control company.'

Have you a seagull story to share? Leave a comment here.

'Smug' swans attack Dalmatian

Feathers fly as dog attacks swans in Hampstead Heath pond

By Tan Parsons

A DOG GOT more than he bargained for after lunging at a pair of swans on Hampstead Heath.

The young Dalmatian leapt into Hampstead's number-one pond at 6pm last Thursday to retrieve a stick thrown by his owner.

But he then made a beeline for the passing bird.

Ron Vester, who lives in Belsize Park, was passing when the attack happened and caught the scrap in the dramatic series of photographs shown on this page.

He said: 'I was just walking by and I heard this piercing sound and I thought, "What the heck is that irritating noise?"

'I looked over and I saw this Dalmatian lunge at the swan. There were eight young cygnets just behind it.

'The two swans started attacking the dog. It went underwater and they covered it with their wings – I thought it was going to drown.

'The dog eventually surfaced and fled looking really uncomfortable. His eyes were really red and it looked like he'd had a really terrible experience. The swans looked really smug.'

The eight cygnets produced this year is a record for Hampstead Heath and it is believed the parents were desperately protecting the young.

Mr Vester continued: 'The dog's owners were freaking out. They didn't know that you shouldn't throw a stick in the water where there is new life. It's terrible but this is a regular occurrence.

'Three swans have been killed by dogs on the heath in the last two or three years.'

A spokeswoman for the City of London Corporation, which manages Hampstead Heath, said she had not heard about the incident. She added: 'A dog is allowed to be off its lead unless it appears to be out of control.

'I don't think anybody could argue that a dog going after swans is not out of control and it would only be common sense for the owners to put it back on the lead at that stage.'

Camden Council recently introduced a series of new dog-control measures in parks and public spaces.

One of the new rules means owners have to put pets on leads if instructed to do so by park wardens.

News   Sport   Lifestyle   Community

Wednesday 29 June 2011

You are here News > Local News

Trapped seagull saved by firefighters

Published on **Monday 1 July 2002 09:51**

A SEAGULL was rescued in a tricky operation from a roof by firefighters last Friday.

The seagull, named Steven by his rescuers, had been trapped on a block of flats in The Bourne for two days after his wing got stuck under the tiles.

Concerned residents raised the alarm and Steven's ordeal was quickly ended.

Firefighters Wally Wallbank and Mike Holloway went up the 30 feet on a turntable ladder to free the bird.

Firefighter Holloway said: "It took two of us to get him down - he put up quite a struggle.

"I held his free wing while the other firefighter got the trapped wing out."

Safely down, Steven was handed over to the RSPCA, but he should make a full recovery.

🔂 SHARE ▪ ▪ ✉ _   ▣ Email to a friend   🖨 Print this page

Trapped seagull saved by firefighters

A SEAGULL WAS rescued in a tricky operation from a roof by firefighters last Friday.

The seagull, named Steven by his rescuers, had been trapped on a block of flats in The Bourne for two days after his wing got stuck under the tiles.

Concerned residents raised the alarm and Steven's ordeal was quickly ended.

Firefighters Wally Wallbank and Mike Holloway went up the 30 feet on a turntable ladder to free the bird.

Firefighter Holloway said: 'It took two of us to get him down – he put up quite a struggle.

'I held his free wing while the other firefighter got the trapped wing out.'

Safely down, Steven was handed over to the RSPCA, but he should make a full recovery.

News   **Sport**   **Lifestyle**   **Community**

Wednesday 29 June 2011

You are here News > Local News

Ungrateful cow snubs rescuers

Published on **Tuesday 14 August 2007 12:02**

An ungrateful cow snubbed two firecrews who raced to rescue it from a ditch.

The bovine was spotted stuck in a ditch just off Harley Shute Road yesterday evening at around 6.45pm.

Passers-by called the emergency services and a special animal rescue unit was called from Crowborough to help the local fire crews.

However, as soon as the animal saw the fuss it was creating it walked out of the ditch all on its own.

East Sussex Fire and Rescue Service said the cow moved itself almost as soon as it saw the firefighters.

A spokeswoman said: "Maybe it didn't like the look of them."

⊕ SHARE ◼ ⬚ ✉ ..   ☞ Email to a friend   🖨 Print this page

Ungrateful cow snubs rescuers

UNGRATEFUL COW SNUBBED two fire crews who raced to rescue it from a ditch.

The bovine was spotted stuck in a ditch just off Harley Shute Road yesterday evening at around 6.45pm.

Passers-by called the emergency services and a special animal rescue unit was called from Crowborough to help the local fire crews.

However, as soon as the animal saw the fuss it was creating it walked out of the ditch all on its own.

East Sussex Fire and Rescue Service said the cow moved itself almost as soon as it saw the firefighters.

A spokeswoman said: 'Maybe it didn't like the look of them.'

Spike the cat has died.

'Celebrity' cat loses life

A POPULAR Lichfield puss has passed on to moggie heaven. Spike the cat lived with her owner Elaine Price in Levetts Fields for nearly nine years and rapidly became something of a 'celebrity' in the street.

"Many people use the route to access the city centre and Spike greeted everyone warmly," said Mrs Price.

"Lots of people spent a few minutes enjoying her company. "Spike would be stroked by adults and children alike and then everyone would carry on their journey with a smile on their face." Sadly the striking black cat with time for everyone died in June and her owners now want to relay the news to all those who petted her. "Spike became quite a celebrity in the street and we would like to let people know as she will be greatly missed," added Mrs Price.

"During the winter when we were at work she would scratch on the Citizens Advice Bureau door and be let in for the day where she would be pampered.

"One night she didn't come home and the next morning, after leafleting the street, she appeared having been locked in the CAB all night.

"It was near Christmas and we then received a Christmas card addressed to 'Spike and family'."

Tributes as popular Lichfield cat dies

A POPULAR LICHFIELD puss has passed on to moggie heaven.

Spike the cat lived with her owner Elaine Price in Levetts Fields for nearly nine years and rapidly became something of a 'celebrity' in the street.

'Many people use the route to access the city centre and Spike greeted everyone warmly,' said Mrs Price.

'Lots of people spent a few minutes enjoying her company.

'Spike would be stroked by adults and children alike and then everyone would carry on their journey with a smile on their face.'

Sadly the striking black cat with time for everyone died in June and her owners now want to relay the news to all those who petted her.

'Spike became quite a celebrity in the street and we would like to let people know as she will be greatly missed,' added Mrs Price.

'During the winter when we were at work she would scratch on the Citizens Advice Bureau door and be let in for the day where she would be pampered.

'One night she didn't come home and the next morning, after leafleting the street, she appeared – having been locked in the CAB all night.

'It was near Christmas and we then received a Christmas card addressed to "Spike and family".'

The Argus

News | Sport | Albion | The Guide | Magazine | Photos | Families | Announcements |

Archive

The Argus » Archive »

ARCHIVE - SATURDAY, 23 JANUARY 2010

Witches blamed for Sussex horse plaits

By Ben Parsons, Crime Reporter »

Witchcraft could be behind a spate of mysterious plaits in horses' manes which has left police baffled.

At least ten horse-owners in Sussex have reported finding plaits in their horses' manes over the last two months.

Police have received reports from places as far apart as Westergate in Chichester, Rother and East Grinstead - reflecting similar reports across the country.

Officers in Dorset have been contacted by a warlock, or male witch, who claimed the plaits are used in rituals by followers of "knot magick", also known as "cord magick".

Witches blamed for Sussex horse plaits

But Kevin Carlyon, the Hastings-based self-proclaimed High Priest of British White Witches, told The Argus some plaits or knots could be evidence of devil-worship or black magic.

He said mostly the practice by "white witches" is harmless and intended for the witch to benefit from the horse's natural power or as a gift or tribute if they see horses as sacred animals.

Mr Carlyon said plaiting has also been known to precede ritual mutilation of horses in black magic.

Mr Carlyon said: "It still goes on unfortunately.

"If it is normal plaiting, like a girl's hair, that is beneficial witchcraft.

"With more complex, more tightly knotted plaits, you're looking down the darker side.

"It is like they are marking the horse to say, this is our chosen one."

PC Peter Child said the possibility of witchcraft has not previously been considered as part of the Sussex Police investigation.

Police are urging people to contact police if their animals have been plaited, and to challenge strangers hanging around farms or places where horses are kept.

Anyone with information about the plaiting is asked to call PC Child on 0845 6070999.

Witches blamed for Sussex horse plaits

By Ben Parsons

WITCHCRAFT COULD BE behind mysterious plaits in horses' manes, which have baffled police.

At least ten horse owners in Sussex have reported finding plaits in their horses' manes over the past two months.

Police have received reports from places as far apart as Westergate in Chichester, Rother and East Grinstead – reflecting similar reports across the country.

Officers in Dorset have been contacted by a warlock, or male witch, who claimed the plaits were used in rituals by followers of 'knot or cord magick'.

But Kevin Carlyon, the Hastings-based self-proclaimed High Priest of British White Witches, told the *Argus* some plaits or knots could be evidence of devil worship or black magic.

He said the practice by 'white witches' was generally harmless and intended for the witch to benefit from the horse's natural power or as a gift or tribute if they saw horses as sacred.

Mr Carlyon said plaiting has also been known to precede ritual mutilation of horses in black magic. He said: 'It still goes on, unfortunately. If it is normal plaiting, like a girl's hair, that is beneficial witchcraft. With more complex, more tightly knotted plaits, you're looking down the darker side. It is like they are marking the horse to say "this is our chosen one".'

Sussex Police's Farm Watch, which offers crime prevention advice in rural areas, warned owners and rural communities to be on guard amid fears the bizarre finds are rustlers' signals marking animals for theft.

None of the plaited horses has been stolen.

It is believed the horses have all been in paddocks or fields when the plaits have been done.

The 54-year-old proprietor of one riding stables spoke to the *Argus* but asked not to be named for fear of becoming a victim. He said footpaths crossing much of the countryside brought people close to horses that were not being watched over.

He said: 'It happened here a month before Christmas. Two horses had plaits put in their tails. The trouble is if the weather is nice you get odd people coming out.'

Police are urging people to call them if their animals have been plaited and to challenge strangers hanging round near horses.

Crabs attack in Hampton

EXHAUSTION BLAMED FOR HERTFORDSHIRE FISH DEATH

Environment

Car hits hedge

A WOMAN escaped without injuries after the car she was driving ran into a hedge in West Cornwall yesterday. The crash, which did not involve any other vehicles, happened in St John's Close, Helston, at about 11.45am. The woman did not need any hospital treatment.

Car hits hedge

A WOMAN ESCAPED without injuries after the car she was driving ran into a hedge in West Cornwall yesterday. The crash, which did not involve any other vehicles, happened in St John's Close, Helston, at about 11.45am. The woman did not need any hospital treatment.

Norwich
Evening News 24

| Home | News | Sport | What's on | Life Matters | Buy and sell | Norwich life |

| Business | Weather | Travel | Derek James | Stacia Briggs | Campaigns | Local life | Fuel prices | Schools |

homes24
jobs24
drive24
mydate24
myphotos24
familynotices24
MyMoney 24
MyVouchers24

UPDATED: Snow on Dereham shop roof still hanging on

Monday, November 29, 2010
12:14 PM

Recommend · Tweet 0

Some of the over-hanging snow on a shop roof in Dereham is still clinging on three days later, remaining a threat to passing shoppers.

Over-hanging snow on the roof of Edinburgh Woollen Mill in Dereham.

Your view · Email · Print · Got a story?

UPDATED: Snow on Dereham shop roof still hanging on

The white mass, which captured readers on EDP24 earlier this week, has significantly reduced in size after large chunks relinquished hold of the Edinburgh Woollen Mill on the towns High Street.

The snow came down in two separate avalanches when there was luckily no one standing underneath.

A notice, put out on the pavements by the shops staff, had warned passersby to beware.

The remaining lump of snow is stubbornly holding on in the corner. People who have spent days watching it from nearby shops and offices have almost given up hope of it ever falling.

Original story published on EDP24 on Monday November 29:

A menacing looking lump of snow on a shop roof in Dereham is giving shoppers cause for concern.

As they negotiate the sludge-covered High Street, townsfolk are being warned of a large accumulation of snow above their heads.

Staff at the Edinburgh Woollen Mill have put a notice on the pavement warning people to beware - over-hanging snow on roof.

Keep checking this website to find out if and when it drops.

Share |

Updated: snow on Dereham shop roof still hanging on

SOME OF THE overhanging snow on a shop roof in Dereham is still clinging on three days later, remaining a threat to passing shoppers.

The white mass, which captured readers on EDP24 earlier this week, has significantly reduced in size after large chunks relinquished hold of the Edinburgh Woollen Mill on the town's High Street.

The snow came down in two separate avalanches when there was luckily no one standing underneath.

A notice, put out on the pavement by the shop's staff, had warned passers-by to beware.

The remaining lump of snow is stubbornly holding on in the corner. People who have spent days watching it from nearby shops and offices have almost given up hope of it ever falling.

Original story published on EDP24 on Monday November 29:

A menacing-looking lump of snow on a shop roof in Dereham is giving shoppers cause for concern.

As they negotiate the sludge-covered High Street, townsfolk are being warned of a large accumulation of snow above their heads.

Staff at the Edinburgh Woollen Mill have put a notice on the pavement warning people to beware – overhanging snow on roof.

Keep checking this website to find out if and when it drops.

Guides delighted with their rubbish award

GUIDES in Ventnor have been rewarded for collecting eight bags of rubbish as part of a campaign to clear litter from the countryside.

Members of the 1st Ventnor guides took part in the IW branch of the Campaign to Protect Rural England's (CPRE-IW) Stop the Drop.

Around 20 guides spent around two hours clearing litter from Grove Road, Ventnor, near St Catherine's School, as well as fields in the area known as The Cut.

John Langley, chairman of the CPRE-IW, held a presentation at the girl-guiding centenary celebration at Corf Camp, Porchfield, where Julie Hudleston, of the 1st Ventnor guides, received a certificate and £100.

"I couldn't believe how enthusiastic the girls were to collect rubbish and it was a great effort to clear so much," said Julie.

● A two-page special, marking 100 years of guiding and the centenary celebrations. See *Weekender*, pages 3 and 4.

Getting their award are, from left, 1st Ventnor guides Maria Snow, 13, Lucy Godden, 14, Ella Granville, 12, Jasmine Pestell, 15, Elizabeth Burton, 13, and leader Julie Hudleston receiving a certficate from CPRE-IW chairman John Langley for their cleaning-up job. 0909-L36919

Guides delighted with their rubbish award

GUIDES IN VENTNOR have been rewarded for collecting eight bags of rubbish as part of a campaign to clear litter from the countryside.

Members of the 1st Ventnor guides took part in the IW branch of the campaign to Protect Rural England's (CPRE-IW) Stop the Drop.

Around 20 guides spent around two hours clearing litter from Grove Road, Ventnor, near St Catherine's School, as well as fields in the area known as The Cut.

John Langley, chairman of the CPRE-IW, held a presentation at the girl-guiding centenary celebration at Corf Camp, Porchfield, where Julie Hudleston, of the 1st Ventnor guides, received a certificate and £100.

'I couldn't believe how enthusiastic the girls were to collect rubbish and it was a great effort to clear so much,' said Julie.

The Arran Voice Ltd Pier Buildings, Brodick, Isle of Arran KA27 8AX

News in Brief...

Arran still in Cunninghame North

Arran will remain part of Cunninghame North constituency, though a planned rejig of electoral boundaries has been released by the Boundary Commission for Scotland. Labour seems likely to lose at least two seats from the process, as Scotland's growing suburbs and commuter towns are altering the existing urban area boundaries. It is proposed that the Glasgow area will have one less seat, while an extra seat goes to the north-east of Scotland. The proposals have caused anger among opposition MSPs and commentators, some of whom have described them as 'crazy' and 'perverse.' Others have interpreted the changes as good old-fashioned gerrymandering, though a substantial proportion are happy with the outlook.

Anyone who had hoped there might be scope for a shift in local authority boundaries will have to wait for some years, as part of the frozen Council Tax deal is an undertaking to leave local boundaries unchanged for the time being.

The public consultation document on electoral boundaries is out for one month and can be found at:
http://www.bcomm-scotland.gov.uk

Arran still in Cunninghame North

ARRAN WILL REMAIN part of Cunninghame North constituency, though a planned rejig of electoral boundaries has been released by the Boundary Commission for Scotland.

Labour seems likely to lose at least two seats from the process, as Scotland's growing suburbs and commuter towns are altering the existing urban area boundaries. It is proposed that the Glasgow area will have one less seat, while an extra seat goes to the north-east of Scotland. The proposals have caused anger among opposition MSPs and commentators, some of whom have described them as 'crazy' and 'perverse'. Others have interpreted the changes as good old-fashioned gerrymandering, though a substantial proportion are happy with the outlook.

Anyone who had hoped there might be scope for a shift in local authority boundaries will have to wait for some years, as part of the frozen Council Tax deal is an undertaking to leave local boundaries unchanged for the time being.

The public consultation document on electoral boundaries is out for one month and can be found at: http://www.bcomm-scotland.gov.uk.

Exeter streets get a brush up as leaves fall

Woman, 79, has to cut verges

Is bridge too nice for Stoke-on-Trent?

Emergencies

Small fire in oven

A small fire in an oven was extinguished before fire-fighters arrived in the early hours of Saturday.

Two crews from Earlham and one from Norwich plus an aerial ladder platform attended the blaze just after midnight in Darrell Place, Earlham.

Small fire in oven

A SMALL FIRE in an oven was extinguished before firefighters arrived in the early hours of Saturday.

Two crews from Earlham and one from Norwich plus an aerial ladder platform attended the blaze just after midnight in Darrell Place, Earlham.

Fire at Rooney favourite Welsh chippy

A NORTH Wales chippy where Wayne Rooney once enjoyed a jumbo sausage and chips was slightly damaged yesterday after a fryer overheated.

Firefighters from Bala and Llangollen were called at 8.30am yesterday morning after reports of a blaze at Y Badell Aur chippy in Bala, Gwynedd.

It was there that Manchester United's first team spent £175 on chips, fish, pies and sausages on an unscheduled stop five years ago after being on a team-building

Blaze... Y Badell Aur chippy in Bala where Wayne Rooney and teammates enjoyed a meal on a trip to N.Wales

canoeing and rafting trip along Afon Tryweryn.

Yesterday's blaze was confined to the fryer and did not affect the restaurant.

Owner Siôn Williams said: "The fryer's a bit damaged but we're hoping to be up and running tomorrow.

"Staff had lit the fryer up to clean the filter when it happened.

"I'd like to thank the staff for reacting quickly."

Fire at Rooney favourite Welsh chippy

A NORTH WALES chippy where Wayne Rooney once enjoyed a jumbo sausage and chips was slightly damaged yesterday after a fryer overheated.

Firefighters from Bala and Llangollen were called at 8.30am yesterday morning after reports of a blaze at Y Badell Aur chippy in Bala, Gwynedd.

It was there that Manchester United's first team spent £175 on chips, fish, pies and sausages on an unscheduled stop five years ago after being on a team-building canoeing and rafting trip along Afon Tryweryn.

Yesterday's blaze was confined to the fryer and did not affect the restaurant.

Owner Siôn Williams said: 'The fryer's a bit damaged but we're hoping to be up and running tomorrow.

'Staff had lit the fryer up to clean the filter when it happened.

'I'd like to thank the staff for reacting quickly.'

The Argus

I'm staying, says Murray

Back Page

50p Saturday, May 16 – Sunday, May 17, 2009   theargus.co.uk   EDF Energy Daily Newspaper of the Year

HOMELESS MAN ESCAPES BIN DEATH

by ANDY CHILES

A HOMELESS man sleeping in a bin narrowly escaped death when he was nearly dropped into a waste truck's crusher.

Union leaders have said urgent action is needed to save its members from potentially killing someone.

Officials from the GMB union, which represents all of Brighton and Hove's binmen, demanded that each vehicle sent out to empty communal bins should have an additional member of staff specifically to check bins before they are emptied.

Mark Turner, GMB branch secretary for Brighton and Hove,

TURN TO PAGE 5

Homeless man escapes bin death

A HOMELESS MAN sleeping in a bin narrowly escaped death when he was nearly dropped into a waste truck's crusher.

Union leaders have said urgent action is needed to save its members from potentially killing someone.

Officials from the GMB union, which represents all of Brighton and Hove's binmen, demanded that each vehicle sent out to empty communal bins should have an additional member of staff specifically to check bins before they are emptied.

Cooking nap blaze avoided

AN evening snack almost led to disaster when the cook fell asleep.

Fire crews were called to a home in Tintagel Close, Hemel Hempstead, by neighbours who spotted smoke on Sunday at around 7.20pm.

They discovered burgers left cooking and a man, believed to be drunk, asleep. It took firefighters several attempts to wake him.

A Herts Fire and Rescue spokesman said: "After a few drinks, a late night snack before bed may seem like just what you need, but falling asleep while cooking could be the last thing you ever do.

"If you are peckish after a night out, sometimes ordering a take away might be the safest option."

Cooking nap blaze avoided

AN EVENING SNACK almost led to disaster when the cook fell asleep.

Fire crews were called to a home in Tintagel Close, Hemel Hempstead, by neighbours who spotted smoke on Sunday at around 7.20pm.

They discovered burgers left cooking and a man, believed to be drunk, asleep. It took firefighters several attempts to wake him.

A Herts Fire and Rescue spokesman said: 'After a few drinks, a late-night snack before bed may seem like just what you need, but falling asleep while cooking could be the last thing you ever do.

'If you are peckish after a night out, sometimes ordering a takeaway might be the safest option.'

Lucky escape as car just misses woman

TOWEL CATCHES FIRE

No one injured in accident

Woman stranded when bus was late

Science & Technology

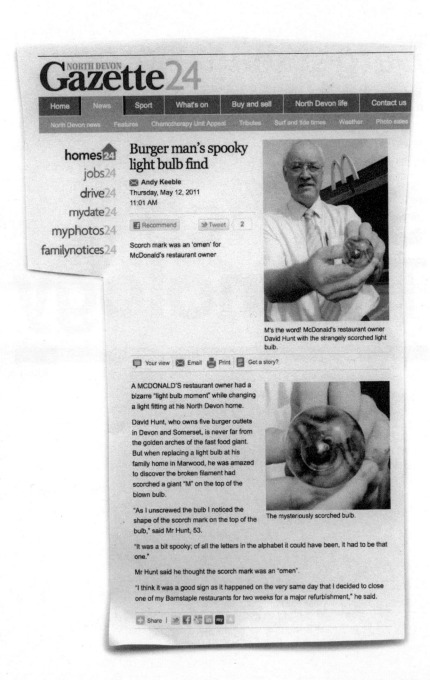

Gazette24

NORTH DEVON

Home | News | Sport | What's on | Buy and sell | North Devon life | Contact us

North Devon news | Features | Chemotherapy Unit Appeal | Tributes | Surf and tide times | Weather | Photo sales

homes24
jobs24
drive24
mydate24
myphotos24
familynotices24

Burger man's spooky light bulb find

✉ Andy Keeble
Thursday, May 12, 2011
11:01 AM

Recommend | Tweet | 2

Scorch mark was an 'omen' for McDonald's restaurant owner

M's the word! McDonald's restaurant owner David Hunt with the strangely scorched light bulb.

Your view | Email | Print | Got a story?

A MCDONALD'S restaurant owner had a bizarre "light bulb moment" while changing a light fitting at his North Devon home.

David Hunt, who owns five burger outlets in Devon and Somerset, is never far from the golden arches of the fast food giant. But when replacing a light bulb at his family home in Marwood, he was amazed to discover the broken filament had scorched a giant "M" on the top of the blown bulb.

"As I unscrewed the bulb I noticed the shape of the scorch mark on the top of the bulb," said Mr Hunt, 53.

The mysteriously scorched bulb.

"It was a bit spooky; of all the letters in the alphabet it could have been, it had to be that one."

Mr Hunt said he thought the scorch mark was an "omen".

"I think it was a good sign as it happened on the very same day that I decided to close one of my Barnstaple restaurants for two weeks for a major refurbishment," he said.

Share |

Burger man's spooky light bulb find

MCDONALD'S RESTAURANT OWNER had a bizarre 'light bulb moment' while changing a light fitting at his North Devon home.

David Hunt, who owns five burger outlets in Devon and Somerset, is never far from the golden arches of the fast food giant. But when replacing a light bulb at his family home in Marwood, he was amazed to discover the broken filament had scorched a giant 'M' on the top of the blown bulb.

'As I unscrewed the bulb I noticed the shape of the scorch mark on the top of the bulb,' said Mr Hunt, 53.

'It was a bit spooky; of all the letters in the alphabet it could have been, it had to be that one.'

Mr Hunt said he thought the scorch mark was an 'omen'.

'I think it was a good sign as it happened on the very same day that I decided to close one of my Barnstaple restaurants for two weeks for a major refurbishment,' he said.

Worthing runaway electric buggy chaos

A WOMAN LOST control of her electric wheelchair in a bank and left two people injured as her buggy ploughed into them.

She tried to drive forward but her buggy suddenly shot off, pinning an elderly woman in front against the counter.

The victim screamed as another customer, Derek Bennett, tried to take control of the wheelchair but it then reversed, ramming him in the shins.

Mr Bennett, of Hawthorn Road, Worthing, was in the queue at Lloyds TSB in South Street, Worthing, when the incident happened.

He said: 'She kept bashing into the perspex partition walls on the way through the queue to the counter. She got to the front and then pushed the button to go forward but the chair roared ahead at full speed and bashed into the counter, hitting an elderly lady who was doing her banking. She must have been in her 80s.'

Mr Bennett, 63, tried to free the trapped woman by lifting up the wheelchair with the lady still in it.

He said: 'She tried to thank me but reversed and knocked into me instead. Then she went forward again and crashed back into the perspex wall.'

The woman crushed against the counter was taken to a seat by her daughter. Bank staff tried to calm her down and offered to send her home in a taxi but her daughter escorted her home.

Mr Bennett said: 'Everybody looked completely shocked.'

He escaped with minor bruising.

Staff at the bank sat with the wheelchair driver and checked she was not injured or too badly shaken up.

She then left to return the wheelchair to the hire shop from which it came.

A Lloyds TSB spokeswoman said its customers' injuries had not been severe following the incident at 1.15pm on Thursday.

Travel

8 DISTRICT NEWS

Lighthouse directions

ANYONE wishing to visit Glas Island lighthouse can walk or drive to the end of the main road where there is a signpost telling them where to turn off.

From there, walk the most following the line of telephone poles.

Lighthouse directions

ANYONE WISHING TO visit Glas Island lighthouse can walk or drive to the end of the main road where there is a signpost telling them where to turn off.

From there walk the coast following the line of telephone poles.

Rescue services alerted to 'witch' out in choppy seas

Swim spells trouble

PICTURES: SAM STEPHENSON

WITCH REPORT: Brighton lifeboat and ambulance crews are called to the aid of charity swimmer Anne Merrett, dressed as a witch, above

WRAPPED UP: Anne safe on shore

by REBECCA EVANS

A WOMAN dressed as a witch was forced to abandon a charity sea swim after risking her life in "gravely hazardous conditions".

Anne Merrett was trying to raise money for Breast Cancer Care by swimming twice around Brighton's Palace Pier.

Her husband feared she was struggling when a balloon tied to her back got detached and he lost sight of her.

Mrs Merrett, 33, had intended for a safety crew in a dinghy to sail next to her but yesterday's conditions were too rough for the boat.

Brighton Lifeboat found her off course about 400 yards out to sea and 200 yards east of the pier.

But Mrs Merrett refused assistance and insisted on swimming to shore.

Lifeboatman Mark Bell said they had not been told about the swim.

He said: "It was gravely hazardous conditions. It was very windy and blowing between 20 and 25 knots, with a one-and-a-half to two metre swell.

"She is entitled to swim if she wants to but it was inappropriate sea conditions to be swimming on your own.

"We came along and offered assistance which she refused. She was a reasonably strong swimmer. There was no immediate danger but if she stayed in for a long time we would be concerned about hypothermia.

"We escorted her back to shore and one of our chaps jumped in and swam with her.

Mrs Merrett said: "My husband did not have faith in me. He thought I was in trouble and called out the RNLI. I was not in trouble. I didn't get into the boat – I swam all the way."

A spokeswoman for South East Coast Ambulance Service said: "We were called out to a 33-year-old woman suffering breathing problems. We were called at 1.16pm and she was treated on the scene."

rebecca.evans
@theargus.co.uk

126

Lifeboat called out to help witch

By Rebecca Evans

A WOMAN DRESSED as a witch was forced to abandon a charity sea swim after risking her life in 'gravely hazardous conditions'.

Anne Merrett was trying to raise money for Breast Cancer Care by swimming twice around Brighton's Palace Pier.

Her husband feared she was struggling when a balloon tied to her back got detached and he lost sight of her.

Mrs Merrett, 53, had intended for a safety crew in a dinghy to sail next to her but yesterday's conditions were too rough for the boat.

Brighton Lifeboat found her off course about 400 yards out to sea and 200 yards east of the pier. But Mrs Merrett refused assistance and insisted on swimming to shore.

Lifeboatman Mark Bell said they had not been told about the swim.

He said: 'It was gravely hazardous conditions. It was very windy and blowing between 20 and 25 knots, with a one-and-a-half to two-metre swell.

'She is entitled to swim if she wants to but it was inappropriate sea conditions to be swimming on your own.

'We came along and offered assistance which she refused. She was a reasonably strong swimmer. There was no immediate danger but if she stayed in for a long time we would be concerned about hypothermia.

'We escorted her back to shore and one of our chaps jumped in and swam with her.'

Mrs Merrett said: 'My husband did not have faith in me. He thought I was in trouble and called out the RNLI. I was not in trouble. I didn't get into the boat – I swam all the way.'

A spokeswoman for South East Coast Ambulance Service said: 'We were called out to a 53-year-old woman suffering breathing problems. We were called at 1.10pm and she was treated on the scene.'

Woman found in Germany

A SANDOWN woman reported missing on a return journey to the Island after a holiday in Poland, has been found safe and well in Germany by Interpol.

Detectives liaised with Interpol to track down the 47-year-old woman, of Broadway, Sandown, who was found in a Berlin hostel on Boxing Day.

Her family reported her missing on December 23, after she lost contact with them for two days.

Woman found in Germany

A SANDOWN WOMAN reported missing on a return journey to the Island after a holiday in Poland, has been found safe and well in Germany by Interpol.

Detectives liaised with Interpol to track down the 47-year-old woman, of Broadway, Sandown, who was found in a Berlin hostel on Boxing Day.

Her family reported her missing on December 23, after she lost contact with them for two days.

The pony express

They said neigh to train ticket for horse... but he tried to take it on anyway

By KATE FORRESTER

STAFF at a train station had a shock when a man turned up and demanded to buy a ticket – for his pony.

And despite being told by Wrexham General's ticket office worker that horses were not allowed on the train, he bundled the creature into a lift and led it onto the platform.

When the train arrived, the man attempted to board it with his four-legged friend, but was stopped by a concerned conductor.

An anonymous source told the Daily Post: "The man took the pony into the ticket office and asked for a ticket. He was refused and told that no horses were allowed on the train.

"But he said 'I know the law' and walked away. He got into a lift with the horse and walked it across the bridge and onto a platform.

"He waited for the train to arrive and then got on himself and was in the process of trying to pull the pony on after him when the conductor stopped him.

"Staff couldn't believe it – most people thought it was a wind-up."

The man is believed to have left the station – with the pony in tow – after a brief argument.

An Arriva Trains Wales spokeswoman said the firm had been made aware of the incident.

"Obviously passengers are not allowed to take livestock on to the train," she added.

"We do allow small animals, such as dogs and guide dogs, onboard but not large animals that could pose a risk to the general public.

"The man was refused a ticket and was not allowed to board the train. He then left the station, so there is no need for any further investigation."

The man tries to buy the horse a ticket (left), takes it in the lift anyway (middle) and then the platform (main, right) before leaving

The pony express

By Kate Forrester

STAFF AT A train station had a shock when a man turned up and demanded to buy a ticket – for his pony.

And despite being told by Wrexham General's ticket office worker that horses were not allowed on the train, he bundled the creature into a lift and led it on to the platform.

When the train arrived, the man attempted to board it with his four-legged friend, but was stopped by a concerned conductor.

An anonymous source told the *Daily Post*: 'The man took the pony into the ticket office and asked for a ticket. He was refused and told that no horses were allowed on the train.

'But he said, "I know the law," and walked away. He got into a lift with the horse and walked it across the bridge and on to a platform.

'He waited for the train to arrive and then got on himself and was in the process of trying to pull the pony on after him when the conductor stopped him.

'Staff couldn't believe it – most people thought it was a wind-up.'

The man is believed to have left the station – with the pony in tow – after a brief argument.

An Arriva Trains Wales spokeswoman said the firm had been made aware of the incident.

'Obviously passengers are not allowed to take livestock on to the train,' she added.

'We do allow small animals, such as dogs and guide dogs, onboard but not large animals that could pose a risk to the general public.

'The man was refused a ticket and was not allowed to board the train. He then left the station, so there is no need for any further investigation.'

Cat hops into delivery van

By Paul Martin

A FORGETFUL CAT from Bowthorpe may have used one of her nine lives when she managed to stow away and ended up in Peterborough.

Travelling cat Essie went missing from her Norwich home on March 24, only to be found by workers at a business in Peterborough two weeks later, and they contacted the RSPCA.

It is thought that the cat got into a car or lorry, continuing her adventure west of Norwich.

Her surprised owner Linda Mortimer, of Reydon Close, was overjoyed by being reunited with Essie, having received a phone call from the RSPCA at Nuvet, Peterborough. The happy reunion was made possible by Essie's microchip which revealed her owner's contact details to help RSPCA staff find her home.

Ms Mortimer, a staff nurse in intensive care at the Norfolk and Norwich University Hospital, has three children – Emily, 15, Edward, 14 and Fiona, 12. She also has two other cats, Storm and Sweep.

She said: 'I was amazed she had got as far as Peterborough. Essie does get lost sometimes, however normally when she wanders off, my two other cats find her and bring her home.

'She went missing last year and was gone from September until November, but she stayed local and our vet found her.

'I think she goes out and forgets where she lives, but how she got into someone's car or van I don't know.'

She added: 'I was so relieved when I received the call to say she had been found safe, the children were so pleased.'

RSPCA Animal Welfare Officer Kathy Hornig said: 'The RSPCA are always keen to urge people to get their pets' microchipped. It is a miracle that Essie has been reunited with her family after venturing so far afield.'

Ms Mortimer added: 'I've had all three of my cats microchipped and it has saved Essie twice now. I don't think we would have found her this time otherwise.'

Essie is now safely back at home.

For more information on microchipping visit the RSPCA website at www.rspca.org.uk.

Town nearly had trams

BLIND GRANNY'S TAXI NIGHTMARE

Motorists face a clear journey home this evening

ROAD STAYS OPEN

Black cat seen near M6

RAIDERS LEAVE INCONTINENCE PADS ON LORRY

Education

The Argus, Wednesday, October 28, 2009

NEWS

Woman is terrified by naked students

NAKED students surrounded and frightened a lone woman after a drunken sports team initiation.

Police said the victim was afraid she was going to be sexually assaulted when 20 jeering men passed her between them, rubbing themselves against her.

The mob, who crossed the University of Sussex campus after a drinking session at a student bar, are being warned the police investigation could land them on the sex offenders' register.

The university condemned those involved and pledged to take disciplinary action.

Inspector Bill Whitehead, of Sussex Police, said: "Regardless of where it has happened and who is

by BEN PARSONS
Crime Reporter

involved, it is outrageous, drunken, yobbish behaviour we are not prepared to tolerate within Brighton and Hove.

"There is a real message that needs to be sent to these people about the standard of decency that is expected of everybody within the city. This poor student did wonder, 'What exactly is going to happen to me? Am I about to be molested by these 20 drunken men?'"

University security guards called police and escorted the 21-year-old woman home.

The attack happened at about 9.30pm on Thursday.

Police said they are treating it for

the moment as a prank that went too far but the attack was recorded as any other crime report and officers have not ruled out more serious action if the evidence is there.

They are looking at CCTV footage and believe they have the names of everybody involved.

The University of Sussex released a statement saying: "Our first concern has been for the welfare of the victim, who was offered immediate aid by our 24-hour security team and is being provided with all necessary support and assistance.

"The university condemns the appalling behaviour of these mindless individuals.

"We are working closely with the police to provide all the information they need to consider what legal

steps they can pursue. Subject to those decisions by the police, we will pursue this matter internally, looking at disciplinary action against the individuals involved and, with the Students Union, strict sanctions on the club concerned."

The university said safety measures including CCTV and 24-hour security were in place.

The statement said: "All universities sadly face the problem of ensuring the safe management of welcome events run by student societies.

"We have been working very closely with our Students' Union to make sure events at Sussex are managed and run safely and responsibly by the student societies."

ben.parsons
@theargus.co.uk

Woman is terrified by naked students

By Ben Parsons

NAKED STUDENTS SURROUNDED and frightened a lone woman after a drunken sports team initiation.

Police said the victim was afraid she was going to be sexually assaulted when 20 jeering men passed her between them, rubbing themselves against her.

The mob, who crossed the University of Sussex campus after a drinking session at a student bar, are being warned the police investigation could land them on the sex offenders' register.

The university condemned those involved and pledged to take disciplinary action.

Inspector Bill Whitehead, of Sussex Police, said: 'Regardless of where it has happened and who is involved, it is outrageous, drunken, yobbish behaviour we are not prepared to tolerate within Brighton and Hove.

'There is a real message that needs to be sent to these people about the standard of decency that is expected of everybody within the city. This poor student did wonder, 'What exactly is going to happen to me? Am I about to be molested by these 20 drunken men?"

University security guards called police and escorted the 21-year-old woman home.

The attack happened at about 9.30pm on Thursday.

Police said they are treating it for the moment as a prank that went too far but the attack was recorded as any other crime report and officers have not ruled out more serious action if the evidence is there.

They are looking at CCTV footage and believe they have the names of everybody involved.

The University of Sussex released a statement saying: 'Our first concern has been for the welfare of the victim, who was offered immediate aid by our 24-hour security team and is being provided with all necessary support and assistance.

'The university condemns the appalling behaviour of these mindless individuals.

'We are working closely with the police to provide all the information they need to consider what legal steps they can pursue. Subject to those decisions by the police, we will pursue this matter internally, looking at disciplinary action against the individuals involved and, with the Students' Union, strict sanctions on the club concerned.'

The university said safety measures including CCTV and 24-hour security were in place.

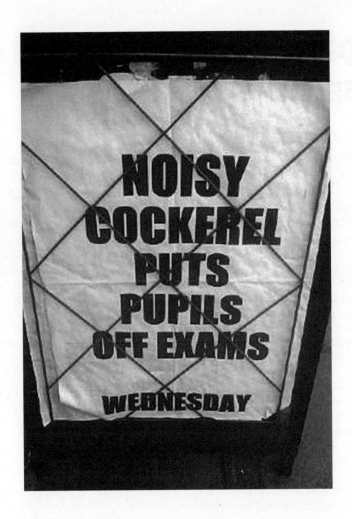

NOISY COCKEREL PUTS PUPILS OFF EXAMS

WEDNESDAY

Noisy cockerel puts pupils off exams

By Raymond Brown

BARRY THE NOISY cockerel has been banished from a Cambridge care home because he disturbs pupils taking exams next door.

The bird has now 'gone on holiday' to Barton after teachers at the Perse School complained his crowing sessions were distracting pupils.

Allan Challis, who looks after Barry, decided to send him on holiday to his friend's pub until the exam season is over.

Barry, a Pekin cockerel named after singer Barry White, was hatched in an incubator at the St George Court care home in Russell Street, Trumpington, last year.

Allan said: 'My mum is a resident at St George's care home and they asked if I could get some chicks. When Barry hatched he was pure white and they wanted him. I told them he was a cockerel and would be noisy, but they fell in love with him. He's named after Barry White but he's gone all colours now. He has three 'wives' who share the coop with him.'

In Barton, Barry has 250 pullets to keep him company, thanks to Allan's friend, Dave Saby, a keen chicken keeper and landlord of The Hoops pub.

Dave said: 'He's not that noisy and he loves it here. The customers are amused by it all, and Barry is happy. He asked me to post a card to the home for him to let them all know he arrived safely.'

Fed up dinner lady quits

SCHOOL SHUT BOY IN SMALL ROOM

Health

MAIN EDITION

The Gazette

Wolstenholme
signs
tel. 01253
403404

WEDNESDAY, OCTOBER 13, 2010   Chilean miners rescue latest - Page 6   45p

Bosses order men to lose weight – or face year suspended

TOO FAT TO DRIVE A BUS

TWO Blackpool bus drivers have been suspended – for being too fat.

Unions bosses today told The Gazette how drivers had been sent home and ordered to lose 7lbs by next month – or their pay will be docked.

Colleagues at Blackpool

EXCLUSIVE
By HELEN STEEL

bus depot said the drivers had been warned if they do not shed the weight they face losing pay for up to a year.

John Boughton, Unite regional industrial organiser, said: "There are currently

two men suspended, with full pay, who have been told they need to lose 7lbs in the next four weeks.

"If they haven't lost this weight in this time, they have been told they will go on unpaid suspension for 12 months. We are currently dealing with this internally.

■ TO PAGE TWO

SUSPENSION THREAT: Two Blackpool Transport bus drivers have been ordered to lose weight

Too fat to drive a bus

By Helen Steel

TWO BLACKPOOL BUS drivers have been suspended – for being too fat.

Unions bosses today told the *Gazette* how drivers had been sent home and ordered to lose 7lbs by next month – or their pay will be docked.

Colleagues at Blackpool bus depot said the drivers had been warned if they do not shed the weight they face losing pay for up to a year.

John Boughton, Unite regional industrial organiser, said: 'There are currently two men suspended, with full pay, who have been told they need to lose 7lbs in the next four weeks.

'If they haven't lost this weight in this time, they have been told they will go on unpaid suspension for 12 months. We are currently dealing with this internally.'

The Argus

50p Saturday, September 19 – Sunday, September 20, 2009 | EDF Energy Daily Newspaper of the Year

SCHOOLBOY TURNS INTO GIRL

A SCHOOLBOY has started the new term as a girl, after changing gender during the summer holidays.

The 12-year-old, from Sussex, attended school in a dress with long hair in pigtails, according to The Sun.

by EMILY-ANN ELLIOTT

The child's name had also been changed to a female one by deed poll and it is believed the pupil is preparing for sex-change surgery.

Teachers at the secondary school were forced to hold an emergency assembly to break the news to other pupils.

However, angry parents criticised the way the situation was handled and said their children were upset and confused by the announcement.

They said failure to inform

TURN TO PAGE 5

Boy, 12, turns into girl

By Emily-Ann Elliott

A SCHOOLBOY HAS started the new term as a girl, after changing gender during the summer holidays.

The 12-year-old, from Sussex, attended school in a dress with long hair in pigtails, according to the *Sun*.

The child's name had also been changed to a female one by deed poll and it is believed the pupil is preparing for sex-change surgery.

Teachers at the secondary school were forced to hold an emergency assembly to break the news to other pupils.

However, angry parents criticised the way the situation was handled and said their children were upset and confused by the announcement.

Yawning almost killed man

By Ben Parsons

A YAWNING HUSBAND almost died after his mouth got stuck wide open.

Dead-tired Ben Shire was making a cup of tea to help keep him awake when a massive yawn took hold and he strained his jaw so much he dislocated it.

The horrified store worker, 34, of Horsham, collapsed in his kitchen unable to breathe or swallow.

His frantic wife dialled 999 as he lay on the floor choking on his saliva and watching his life pass before his eyes.

Paramedics rushed him to hospital with his jaw still locked open where medics brought him back from the brink of death using a suction device.

Doctors battled for four hours with Ben, a father of three, to close his gaping mouth.

He said the incident was no laughing matter and he could easily have choked to death.

He told the *Argus*: 'We can laugh about it now, but it wasn't funny at the time.

'I couldn't breathe because I was choking – it felt like two fingers down my throat.

'The more I panicked, the more I struggled for breath.'

His wife Sam, a hotel cleaner, added: 'I was really panicking and didn't know what to do.'

A spokesman for East Surrey Hospital in Redhill, where doctors reset Ben's jaw, praised the quick-thinking actions of the ambulance crew.

Cases of people's jaws locking mid-yawn are very rare.

Doctors advise people who do experience the problem to bend forward or lie on their side in the recovery position to let gravity ease the pressure.

People with jaws locked open can feel like they are choking because of the build-up of saliva in their mouths.

To push a locked-open jaw back into place dentists push the lower jaw downwards and back by pushing on the lower back teeth.

The condition known as lockjaw – where the jaw sets shut – is more commonly associated with the early stages of tetanus.

This is followed by stiffness in the neck, problems swallowing, rigid abdominal muscles, spasms, sweating and fever.

Lovesick student broke into morgue with axe

By Emily-Ann Elliott

A LOVESTRUCK STUDENT smashed his way into a mortuary with an axe because he feared the girl he fancied had died.

Panic-stricken Benjamin Barton spent about 90 minutes examining corpses and scouring confidential records in a bizarre attempt to find out whether she was there.

The 24-year-old had fallen for Amy Ogdon after they met at a Christian Union meeting at Southampton University. But when he and mutual friends could not contact her, he feared the worst.

Barton, from Aldwick, Bognor, went to Southampton General Hospital where he tried to talk his way into the mortuary by claiming to the site manager he was a medical student and had left something to do with his work inside.

The manager took his name and mobile phone number and contacted the out-of-hours mortician who told him he would be let in the following day to collect what he wanted.

Barton left the hospital but only to buy an axe which he used to smash his way through internal doors after kicking in the outside door.

Inside, he carried out a search of confidential records and documents, gained access to the computer system, and looked at bodies, before leaving with two documents and a key to the rest room in the mortuary.

Police were able to trace him through the details he had left earlier with the site manager.

They found the documents, key and axe as well as a chisel and two hammers in his room.

Southampton Crown Court was told Barton's feelings for Ms Ogdon were unrequited and she had a boyfriend.

Barton, who graduated with a first-class degree in complexity science, admitted causing damage estimated to be between £6,000 and £8,000.

In mitigation, Nathan Rasiah said Barton had been an accomplished student who was described as well mannered and trustworthy.

'In no way did he search the mortuary for gratification. He was labouring under the misapprehension that the girl he loved was dead. There was no menace. No violence was directed towards any person.'

Barton was placed under supervision for 12 months on the condition he continued receiving medical help for nine months. He was also ordered to pay £1,000 compensation.

CLOSE SHAVE

A man had a narrow escape from, injury on Monday at around 11.15 a.m. when he was knocked into a hedge alongside Crosthwaite Road by a passing car pulling a caravan. The vehicle did not stop. Police said the local man was not hurt in the incident.

Close shave

A MAN HAD a narrow escape from injury on Monday at around 11.15am when he was knocked into a hedge alongside Crosthwaite Road by a passing car pulling a caravan. The vehicle did not stop. Police said the local man was not hurt in the incident.

Woman swallows spoon

Victims sue over 'toxic sofas'

WORKER
CUTS FINGER

Arts

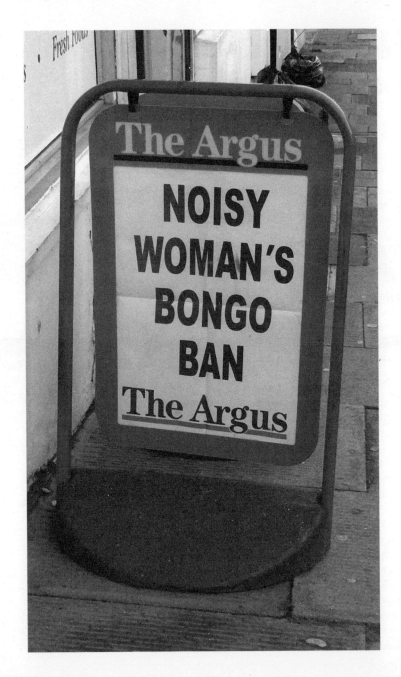

Noisy woman's bongo ban

By Alison Cridland

AN ALCOHOLIC HAS had her drums confiscated.

Unemployed Sharon Nesbitt kept her neighbours awake as she repeatedly drummed into the night.

The 39-year-old was ordered to pay almost £2,000 in fines after she admitted breaching a noise abatement notice.

Brighton Magistrates' Court was told Brighton and Hove City Council served the notice in December last year after complaints about Nesbitt's behaviour.

In February this year she was convicted of breaching the notice for the first time and fined £600 with £750 costs. So far she has not paid any of the money owed.

Nesbitt, of Halland Road, Moulsecoomb, was back in court yesterday for breaching the notice a second time.

The court was told neighbours had suffered from music blasting out of her one-bedroom flat as well as shouting, doors slamming and the noise from her bongos.

Len Batten, prosecuting for the council, told the court after further complaints noise patrol officers went to her home on the night of April 4 and from outside her flat they heard her music.

This time the officers seized her music equipment, along with DVDs, televisions and her bongos.

At an earlier hearing Nesbitt had appealed to the magistrates: 'Keep my possessions but don't take my soul and my bongos.'

But magistrates ordered the equipment to be forfeited and it will not be returned.

Magistrate Dr Susan Iles-Jonas told her: 'This is a very serious charge. The offence affects the lives of your neighbours and this has to stop.'

Stephen Harris, defending, said Nesbitt, a mother of three, suffered from mental health problems and an addiction to alcohol.

He said: 'She found playing the drums a release and it kept her away from drinking alcohol. Since the equipment was seized she has lapsed into greater use of alcohol.'

Magistrates fined her £400 plus a £500 penalty for breaching the order a second time. She was also ordered to pay £840 costs.

Councillor Geoffrey Theobald, the council's cabinet member for environment, said: 'We will not tolerate noise nuisance of any kind and will not hesitate to prosecute those responsible.'

Music equipment seized by the council is given away to charities, schools and non-profit organisations. Anyone interested in receiving the equipment should call the council on 01273 292259.

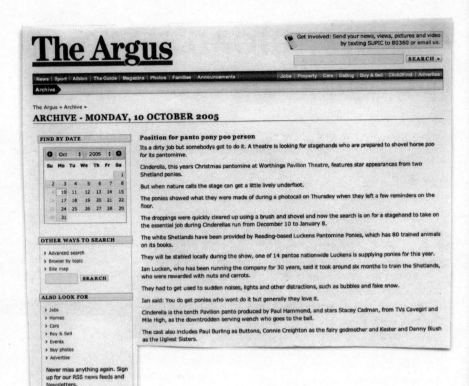

The Argus

News | Sport | Albion | The Guide | Magazine | Photos | Families | Announcements | Jobs | Property | Cars | Dating | Buy & Sell | Click2Find | Advertise

Archive

The Argus » Archive »

ARCHIVE - MONDAY, 10 OCTOBER 2005

FIND BY DATE

Su	Mo	Tu	We	Th	Fr	Sa
						1
2	3	4	5	6	7	8
	10	11	12	13	14	15
16	17	18	19	20	21	22
23	24	25	26	27	28	29
30	31					

OTHER WAYS TO SEARCH

> Advanced search
> Browse by topic
> Site map

SEARCH

ALSO LOOK FOR

> Jobs
> Homes
> Cars
> Buy & Sell
> Events
> Buy photos
> Advertise

Never miss anything again. Sign up for our RSS news feeds and Newsletters.

Position for panto pony poo person

Its a dirty job but somebodys got to do it. A theatre is looking for stagehands who are prepared to shovel horse poo for its pantomime.

Cinderella, this years Christmas pantomine at Worthings Pavilion Theatre, features star appearances from two Shetland ponies.

But when nature calls the stage can get a little lively underfoot.

The ponies showed what they were made of during a photocall on Thursday when they left a few reminders on the floor.

The droppings were quickly cleared up using a brush and shovel and now the search is on for a stagehand to take on the essential job during Cinderellas run from December 10 to January 8.

The white Shetlands have been provided by Reading-based Luckens Pantomine Ponies, which has 80 trained animals on its books.

They will be stabled locally during the show, one of 14 pantos nationwide Luckens is supplying ponies for this year.

Ian Lucken, who has been running the company for 30 years, said it took around six months to train the Shetlands, who were rewarded with nuts and carrots.

They had to get used to sudden noises, lights and other distractions, such as bubbles and fake snow.

Ian said: You do get ponies who wont do it but generally they love it.

Cinderella is the tenth Pavilion panto produced by Paul Hammond, and stars Stacey Cadman, from TVs Cavegirl and Mile High, as the downtrodden serving wench who goes to the ball.

The cast also includes Paul Burling as Buttons, Connie Creighton as the fairy godmother and Kester and Danny Blush as the Ugliest Sisters.

Position for panto pony poo person

IT'S A DIRTY job but somebody's got to do it. A theatre is looking for stagehands who are prepared to shovel horse poo for its pantomime.

Cinderella, this year's Christmas pantomine at Worthing's Pavilion Theatre, features star appearances from two Shetland ponies.

But when nature calls the stage can get a little lively underfoot.

The ponies showed what they were made of during a photocall on Thursday when they left a few reminders on the floor.

The droppings were quickly cleared up using a brush and shovel and now the search is on for a stagehand to take on the essential job during *Cinderella*'s run from December 10 to January 8.

The white Shetlands have been provided by Reading-based Luckens Pantomine Ponies, which has 80 trained animals on its books.

They will be stabled locally during the show, one of 14 pantos nationwide Luckens is supplying ponies for this year.

Ian Lucken, who has been running the company for 30 years, said it took around six months to train the Shetlands, who were rewarded with nuts and carrots.

They had to get used to sudden noises, lights and other distractions, such as bubbles and fake snow.

Ian said: 'You do get ponies who won't do it but generally they love it.'

Cinderella is the tenth Pavilion panto produced by Paul Hammond, and stars Stacey Cadman, from TV's *Cavegirl* and *Mile High*, as the downtrodden serving wench who goes to the ball.

The cast also includes Paul Burling as Buttons, Connie Creighton as the Fairy Godmother and Kester and Danny Blush as the Ugliest Sisters.

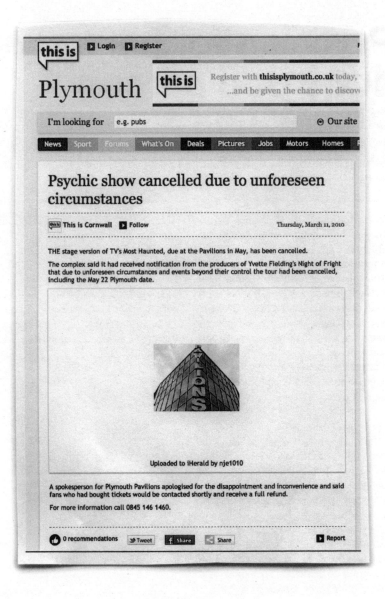

Psychic show cancelled due to unforeseen circumstances

THE STAGE VERSION of TV's *Most Haunted*, due at the Pavilions in May, has been cancelled.

The complex said it had received notification from the producers of Yvette Fielding's *Night of Fright* that due to unforeseen circumstances and events beyond their control the tour had been cancelled, including the May 22 Plymouth date.

A spokesperson for Plymouth Pavilions apologised for the disappointment and inconvenience and said fans who had bought tickets would be contacted shortly and receive a full refund.

Nuns in fight against strippers

By Nigel Freedman

A GROUP OF nuns are fighting plans to allow exotic dancers to perform opposite a convent.

They are backing residents who are against the move by the Broadway nightclub, in Uckfield, which also wants to extend its opening hours.

Nuns at the Society of St Margaret's Convent across the road fear 'immoral' entertainment could lead youngsters into temptation.

Wealden District Council has received letters from more than 70 people objecting to the club's bid to stay open until 2am during the week and 4.30am at weekends and a proposal to stage 'occasional exotic dancing and striptease-to-music' performances.

One resident said: 'The club causes me sleepless nights with thugs throwing bottles and fighting.

'Sex takes place outside our homes and people urinate in the street. We live in fear of what the weekend will bring.'

The convent is a retreat run by nuns where guests go to contemplate in silence.

The convent's Reverend Mother said: 'Licensing adult dancing of a very undesirable type would downgrade Uckfield.

'Teenagers flock past the club after school and are, I am told, already interested and want to go to the club if the dancing is permitted. I do not feel this is what the town should be offering young folk at a vulnerable age.'

Other residents have complained to the council about bottles and condoms littering the streets and of being threatened by revellers in the early hours.

Sussex Police are also objecting to the longer opening hours, saying they have been called to trouble at the club eight times since March last year.

One fight in October involved up to 20 people and an off-duty policeman was assaulted when he tried to stop a fight inside the club last month.

Richard Calderbank, managing director of Ambassador Leisure Services, said the club's door staff worked closely with police.

He said: 'Police have failed to take into consideration how well the club is run and the very few times they have had to attend the club for a serious event.'

The council's licensing sub-committee will discuss the application when it meets on Thursday.

Owners of parrot Seve Ballesteros pay tribute to pet's namesake

Food &
Drink

Whitstable mum in custard shortage

By J. Nurden

A MUM OF three is dis-custard after a hunt for the dessert sauce in the town proved fruitless.

Keen baker Jules Serkin, 43, of West Cliff, Whitstable, needed a tin of custard powder to top off her apple and blackcurrant crumble.

But she was left with a sour taste in her mouth after getting no joy in either Co-ops at Oxford Street and Canterbury Road, and in Somerfield, in the High Street.

Even a trek to Tankerton's Tesco Express – a corner shop version of its superstores – was wasted.

'I try to support my local businesses, but in the end I had to resort to going to one of the big supermarkets to get what I needed,' said Jules, a holiday rental company director.

'I feel very sad that I can't seem to get basic stuff from my high street, and am driven to go online.

'Custard is a staple product on my shopping list and I cannot understand why it should be so hard to find.

'An assistant in Somerfield said they'd had other shoppers asking for tins of custard, but it hadn't been in stock since the shop was refurbished.

'And in the Co-ops I was just greeted with an empty shelf where it should be, and no idea when they might be getting it in.'

'I am upset because it seems these shops cannot order a product that customers are demanding as it doesn't seem to fit in with what they are selling.

'I had to resort to buying sachets which cost only a few pence less than a tin, and don't go very far at all. If I buy a tin, it goes in my pantry and will last me quite a few crumbles.

'I'm making an apple and blackcurrant crumble, and as I am trying to eat healthily can control what I put into the custard, like skimmed milk.

'With the sachets, there are all sorts of ingredients and additives – and you just add water to make it.

'It's very convenient, but not as good as the real thing. Custard should be a lovely comfort, nice and thick.'

Mrs Serkin finally managed to find a tin of own brand custard powder in a Co-op, a few days after her initial hunt, but not her beloved Bird's.

Spokesman for Somerfield Pete Williams said: 'Somerfield in Whitstable High Street underwent a major investment last April to upgrade and improve the store for local customers. 'We are a bit perplexed about your reader's trouble

cont. on page 178

in finding custard in the store. It offers a variety of custards including: tinned, fresh, cartons and in powdered form.

'Today (Monday March 23) it has both Somerfield own brand tinned custard, and tinned custard made by Ambrosia. The store stocks Somerfield Instant Custard Mix – to which you simply add water.

'Regrettably the store does not have sufficient space to stock the larger tins of classic Bird's Custard Powder – to which you add milk and sugar to make your custard.'

A Co-operative Group spokesman said: 'We are sorry to hear a customer is unhappy with our custard range in Whitstable.

'Our smaller convenience store in Canterbury Road has only ever sold sachets of Bird's custard powder.

'The Oxford Street store did stock Bird's tinned custard until recently but the product was withdrawn following

thorough analysis of product sales across our range.

'This store does, however, sell the Co-operative's own brand of tinned custard powder and we would be pleased to offer this customer a free sample to try.'

WHT   visit our website www.thisiskent.co.uk   The Times

Baker's custardy fight after Bird's takes flight

Report by Roger Kasper

roger.kasper@kmmedia.co.uk

A MUM of three is dis-custard after a hunt for the dessert sauce in the town proved fruitless.

Keen baker Jules Serkin, 43, of West Cliff, Whitstable, needed a tin of custard powder to top off her apple and blackcurrant crumble.

But she was left with a sour taste in her mouth after getting no joy in either Co-ops, in Oxford Street and Canterbury Road, or in Somerfield in the High Street.

Even a trek to Tankerton's Tesco Express – a corner shop version of its superstores – was a sticky point.

"I try to support my local businesses, but in the end I had to resort to going to one of the big supermarkets to get what I needed," said Jules, a holiday rental company director.

"I feel very sad that I can't

meet their needs. We are a bit perplexed about your reader's trouble in finding custard in the store.

"It offers a variety of custards including: tinned, fresh, cartons and in powdered form.

"On Monday it had both Somerfield own brand tinned custard and tinned custard made by Ambrosia.

"The store stocks Somerfield Instant Custard Mix to which you simply add water

"Regrettably the store does not have sufficient space to stock the larger tins of classic Bird's Custard Powder – to which you add milk and sugar to make your custard."

A Co-operative Group spokesman said: "We are sorry to hear a customer is unhappy with our custard range in Whitstable

❝ Custard should be a lovely comfort, nice and thick ❞

sachets which cost only a few pence less than a tin, and don't go very far at all. If I buy a tin, it goes in my pantry and will last me quite a few crumbles.

"I'm making an apple and blackcurrant crumble and, as I am trying to eat healthily I can control what I put into the custard, like skimmed milk.

Just desserts: Jules Serkin pudding on a brave face.

Elderly terrified by food fight

Pensioner's breakfast catches fire

FIREFIGHTERS had an early morning wake-up call when a pensioner's breakfast caught fire.

A fire engine from Minehead was called to an elderly persons' complex in Summerland Avenue in the town just before 6am on Tuesday.

On arrival, they found an extremely burned piece of toast and equally blackened toaster.

A spokesman for the brigade said the toast had caught fire, triggering an alarm system and causing minor damage to the toaster.

Pensioner's breakfast catches fire

FIREFIGHTERS HAD AN early morning wake-up call when a pensioner's breakfast caught fire.

A fire engine from Minehead was called to an elderly persons' complex in Summerland Avenue in the town just before 6am on Tuesday.

On arrival, they found an extremely burned piece of toast and equally blackened toaster.

A spokesman for the brigade said the toast had caught fire, triggering an alarm system and causing minor damage to the toaster.

News in Brief

Raiders go nuts

A SECURITY guard on patrol at a building site in Liversedge last week returned to his office to find thieves had stolen ... two packets of peanuts!

The man had been doing his evening rounds at the construction site in Parkin Street when raiders targeted the office. Police believe one packet was salted and the other dry roasted.

A pair of sunglasses, a mobile phone charger plus a pipe and some tobacco were also taken.

Raiders go nuts

A SECURITY GUARD on patrol at a building site in Liversedge last week returned to his office to find thieves had stolen... two packets of peanuts!

The man had been doing his evening rounds at the construction site in Parkin Street when raiders targeted the office. Police believe one packet was salted and the other dry roasted.

A pair of sunglasses, a mobile phone charger plus a pipe and some tobacco were also taken.

Harrogate *Advertiser*

News   **Sport**   **Lifestyle**   **Community**

Friday 1 July 2011

Log in   Register

You are here News > Harrogate, Knaresborough & Nidderdale

Banana drama for Irma

Sponsored by

Published on **Thursday 3 June 2010 13:41**

A HARROGATE pensioner has described the moment she discovered a rare food phenomenon- a straight banana!

Irma Gledhill, 90, of Greenfield Court, Wetherby Road said she was given the oddly shaped fruit after eating dinner one night at her residential home.

"I said, 'Oh, I've got a straight banana! I thought it was a joke," she explained.

"After lunch we all laughed about it and we showed it around. Instead of the usual pudding I asked for fruit.

"It was quite a long straight banana. It was a beautiful yellow to start with but after a while it started to go brown."

Straight bananas hit the news in the 80s when the rumour mill spuriously suggested Brussels wanted to ban the food.

So what is the fate for Mrs Gledhill's banana? "If I can't do anything else, I will eat it," she said.

SHARE   Email to a friend   Print this page

News
Harrogate, Knaresborough & Nidderdale
Letters
Business
Regional
National
Health

TOP STORIES
Thousands stay home as Harrogate teachers strike

Can you identify this woman?

Volunteers lend a hand to 'Love Starbeck'

Rally stage for Harrogate?

Ruling on porn shame councillor

Banana drama for Irma

A HARROGATE PENSIONER has described the moment she discovered a rare food phenomenon – a straight banana!

Irma Gledhill, 90, of Greenfield Court, Wetherby Road, said she was given the oddly shaped fruit after eating dinner one night at her residential home.

'I said, "Oh, I've got a straight banana!" I thought it was a joke,' she explained.

'After lunch we all laughed about it and we showed it around. Instead of the usual pudding I asked for fruit.

'It was quite a long straight banana. It was a beautiful yellow to start with but after a while it started to go brown.'

Straight bananas hit the news in the 80s when the rumour mill spuriously suggested Brussels wanted to ban the food.

So what is the fate for Mrs Gledhill's banana? 'If I can't do anything else, I will eat it,' she said.

Tortoise stolen to sell for booze

A MAN will have to shell out £300 after admitting stealing a rare tortoise from a pet store.

Keith Odgers, 24, appeared before Hartlepool Magistrates' Court after the Horsefield tortoise, worth £100, was stolen from Hartlepool's Stranton Pets, in Vicarage Gardens.

Vickie Wilson, prosecuting, said that on January 13 Odgers walked into the pet shop, took the tortoise from its heated cage and left, concealing it under his jacket.

Magistrates heard Odgers later sold it to buy alcohol.

She said Odgers, from Holt

by **Emma Greenhalgh**

emma.greenhalgh@northeast-press.co.uk

Street, Hartlepool, was caught on CCTV. She said Odgers told officers he "sold it to get blaked" but would not reveal who to.

Mitigating, John Relton urged magistrates to give Odgers credit for his timely guilty plea and the fact that he has no previous convictions for dishonesty.

He said that Odgers' decision to steal was influenced partly by drink and that there was no suggestion of cruelty or mishandling of the animal.

Odgers, who pleaded guilty to stealing the tortoise, was fined

£100 and ordered to pay £100 compensation for the tortoise.

He was ordered to pay costs of £85 and a victim surcharge of £15.

Mavis Austin, 59, who has ran the store with her husband Ken, 63, for seven years, appeared in the *Mail* when the tortoise was taken.

She said at the time that she always had three of that particular type in stock.

She said: "They are a year old and only the size of the palm of your hand and they grow to about 14 inches in length.

"But it is a strange type of theft as I wouldn't imagine a tortoise is something you can go and sell in a pub."

VALUABLE: Pet shop owner Mavis Austin with a similar Horsefield tortoise. *(IRN 492547)*

● Full story: Page 5

MAN STOLE TORTOISE TO PAY FOR BOOZE
SEE PAGE 2

Tortoise stolen to sell for booze

By Emma Greenhalgh

A MAN WILL have to shell out £300 after admitting stealing a rare tortoise from a pet store.

Keith Odgers, 24, appeared before Hartlepool Magistrates' Court after the Horsefield tortoise, worth £100, was stolen from Hartlepool's Stranton Pets, in Vicarage Gardens.

Vickie Wilson, prosecuting, said that on January 13 Odgers walked into the pet shop, took the tortoise from its heated cage and left, concealing it under his jacket.

Magistrates heard Odgers later sold it to buy alcohol.

She said Odgers, from Holt Street, Hartlepool, was caught on CCTV. She said Odgers told officers he 'sold it to get blaked' but would not reveal who to.

Mitigating, John Relton urged magistrates to give Odgers credit for his timely guilty plea and the fact that he has no previous convictions for dishonesty.

He said that Odgers' decision to steal was influenced partly by drink and that there was no suggestion of cruelty or mishandling of the animal.

Odgers, who pleaded guilty to stealing the tortoise, was fined £100 and ordered to pay £100 compensation for the tortoise.

He was ordered to pay costs of £85 and a victim surcharge of £15.

Mavis Austin, 59, who has run the store with her husband Ken, 63, for seven years, appeared in the *Mail* when the tortoise was taken.

She said at the time that she always had three of that particular type in stock.

She said: 'They are a year old and only the size of the palm of your hand, and they grow to about 14 inches in length.

'But it is a strange type of theft as I wouldn't imagine a tortoise is something you can go and sell in a pub.'

Home & Garden

No bin

A NEW grit bin at Keddington Road in Louth will not be provided this winter.

Louth Town Council asked Lincolnshire County Council to provide a bin, but their request did not meet the relevant criteria for a new bin.

No bin

A NEW GRIT bin at Keddington Road in Louth will not be provided this winter.

Louth Town Council asked Lincolnshire County Council to provide a bin, but their request did not meet the relevant criteria for a new bin.

Oven removed from home

Isle of Wight County Press online

CHURCH
TH
VENTNOR,

Search iwcp.co.uk   Go

Home | News | Sport | Features | Entertainment | Info Desk | Contact Us | Advertising | Jo

Obituaries | Business | Wedding Reports | Environment | Video

Home / News /
News

Oven removed from home

By Emily Pearce - Thursday, March 4, 2010

Search iwcp.co.uk: Go

A ST Helens resident called the fire service in the early hours of this morning (Thursday), worried about a burning smell coming from her oven.
Firefighters attended the scene, in Downsview Road, shortly after midnight, and removed the oven from the house.

Reporter: emilyp@iwcpmail.co.uk

LATEST NEWS

- Comedy star attends theatre awards
- Limited train service back in action
- Firefighters in demand as floods hit Island
- School's message to future generations
- Hospital tries special floor to protect elderly
- Care on Island rated highly by watchdog
- Protection for sea and shore
- Skatepark deal 'near'
- Cash for event
- Weather halts repairs to floating bridge repair

More News: 1 - **2** - **3**

Bookmark with: **Delicious** **Digg** **reddit** **Facebook** **StumbleUpon** **Tweet this**

192

Oven removed from home

By Emily Pearce

A ST HELENS resident called the fire service in the early hours of this morning (Thursday), worried about a burning smell coming from her oven.

Firefighters attended the scene, in Downsview Road, shortly after midnight, and removed the oven from the house.

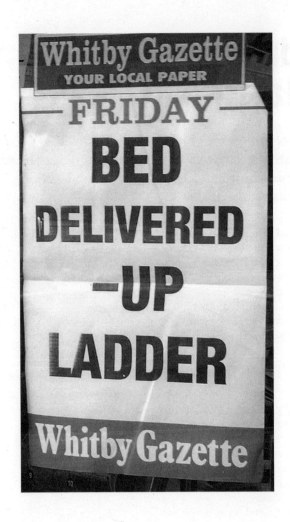

Bed delivered – up ladder

IT WAS FUN and games on Whitby's East Side on Tuesday when Beevers attempted to deliver a double sofa bed to one of Whitby's quaint cottages.

Whitby Gazette reader Maggie Hall ordered the bed from Beevers' Stakesby Vale showroom after she set her heart on it.

But the delivery was not that simple.

Due to the narrow alley leading to her home in Sandgate, the bed was brought down the slipway off Tin Ghaut and hoisted up to the property's tip-and-turn window.

It was then lowered into the property through one of the windows and the old one removed.

The 4ft 6in leather sleep space has very wide arms and a high back.

Maggie said: 'I totally believe in trying to buy items from local businesses and I was so impressed Beevers wanted to help me, despite the obvious architectural barriers posed by Whitby.

'What a service and what a feat – it seems the delivery turned into a great sofa spectator sport.'

Pete Betts, Beevers' store director, said: 'It took four of us to get the bed down the harbourside through all the mud and seaweed.

'We had to climb up some ladders and get it through the window on the balcony.

'This shows the lengths we are prepared to go to in our determination to provide a good quality service and guarantee the delivery of customers' furniture.

'In a place like Whitby this is not rare – we have to perform unusual deliveries like this all the time.'

FREEZER TAKEN

A fridge freezer was taken from the back garden of a house in St Herbert's Street, Keswick, sometime between 9 am and 11 am last Thursday.

Freezer taken

A FRIDGE FREEZER was taken from the back garden of a house in St Herbert's Street, Keswick, sometime between 9am and 11am last Thursday.

New fencing

TUCKTON: Rotting fencing is to be replaced at Tuckton Tea Gardens, Bournemouth council has confirmed.

Parks department staff will replace a 20-metre section with a timber and wire trellis and the area will be replanted with climbing plants.

The work will cost between £700 and £800.

New fencing

TUCKTON: ROTTING FENCING is to be replaced at Tuckton Tea Gardens, Bournemouth council has confirmed.

Parks department staff will replace a 20-metre section with a timber and wire trellis and the area will be replanted with climbing plants.

The work will cost between £700 and £800.

Welsh bungalow has neat garden

Chair destroyed

Sport

The Argus, Monday, May 18, 2009

NEWS

'She was itching to get in but waves were a little high'

Cassie loves being chucked in the sea

Animal cruelty or an over-reaction? Tell us at
theargus.co.uk news

RUFF TREATMENT?
Scott Meredith and his uncle's dog Cassie, right. Below, the photos police say they have studied, along with the RSPCA

by EMILY WALKER

THE man photographed throwing a dog into the sea has dismissed fears of animal cruelty by saying the animal "loves it".

Scott Meredith, 22, of Manor Close, Southwick, was pictured by a passer-by hurling a Staffordshire terrier-cross into the water near Hove Lawns.

Police and the RSPCA launched an investigation into whether his actions constituted animal cruelty.

But unemployed Mr Meredith said: "I don't know what all the fuss is about."

He said he only threw his cousin Adam's dog Cassie into the sea because she was scared to follow his own dog Missy into the waves.

Mr Meredith said: "Missy jumped straight in. Cassie was yelling and itching to get in but the waves were up a little which put her off.

"So I picked her up with one hand under her neck and the other holding her belly and threw her. She loves it and once in the water she was fine.

"She wasn't hurt and I only threw her in the once.

"I'm not worried about the police or RSPCA because I haven't done anything wrong.

"The pictures look like I'm throwing the dog high but only

the angle of the photo makes it look like that.

"Even when I was pulling the dog out of the water, I wasn't being cruel, I was just stopping her from crossing on to a beach where dogs are banned."

Mr Meredith's uncle, who would only give his name as Danny, said the dogs were loved and well looked after.

He said: "I have been down there with the dogs.

"Where that groyne is, one side is 4ft high and the other side 10ft high.

"From where the picture was taken it does look a bit bad.

"But I know Scott and I know the dogs. I have taken them down there myself and they are perfectly well treated.

"If the police were that concerned, why haven't they spoken to him?"

PC Lisa Timerick said she had looked at the pictures and would be taking witness statements before taking matters any further.

emily.walker
@theargus.co.uk

The Argus
DOG THROWER: SHE LOVES IT
The Argus

Dog thrower: she loves it

By Emily Walker

THE MAN PHOTOGRAPHED throwing a dog into the sea has dismissed fears of animal cruelty by saying the animal 'loves it'.

Scott Meredith, 22, of Manor Close, Southwick, was pictured by a passer-by hurling a Staffordshire terrier-cross into the water near Hove Lawns.

Police and the RSPCA launched an investigation into whether his actions constituted animal cruelty.

But unemployed Mr Meredith said: 'I don't know what all the fuss is about.'

He said he only threw his cousin Adam's dog Cassie into the sea because she was scared to follow his own dog Missy into the waves.

Mr Meredith said: 'Missy jumped straight in. Cassie was yelling and itching to get in but the waves were up a little which put her off.

'So I picked her up with one hand under her neck and the other holding her belly and threw her. She loves it and once in the water she was fine.

'She wasn't hurt and I only threw her in the once.

'I'm not worried about the police or RSPCA because I haven't done anything wrong.

'The pictures look like I'm throwing the dog high but only the angle of the photo makes it look like that.

'Even when I was pulling the dog out of the water, I wasn't being cruel. I was just stopping her from crossing on to a beach where dogs are banned.'

Mr Meredith's uncle, who would only give his name as Danny, said the dogs were loved and well looked after.

He said: 'I have been down there with the dogs.

'Where that groyne is, one side is 4ft high and the other side is 10ft high.

'From where the picture was taken it does look a bit bad.

'But I know Scott and I know the dogs. I have taken them down there myself and they are perfectly well treated.

'If the police were that concerned, why haven't they spoken to him?'

Police said they were investigating the incident last week, but have not yet spoken to Mr Meredith.

PC Lisa Timerick said she had looked at the pictures and would be taking witness statements before taking matters any further.

Runners complete marathon

Charities reap the benefit

By **Sam Inkersole**
sam.inkersole@sevenoaks-chronicle.co.uk

THOUSANDS of runners for charity joined the world's athletic elite in the London Marathon at the weekend. The ten competitors from the Sevenoaks area who last week featured in the Chronicle all managed to complete the gruelling 26.2-mile course.

David Hale timed an impressive 3hrs 17mins 47secs, a personal best for the marathon.

He said: "It was another scorcher weather-wise.

"At 12 miles, I was on target for 3hr 10mins.

"I started to feel the quads hurting about 20 miles in but kept my head down and plugged away at what felt like a slow pace but was on a par with everyone around me.

"The atmosphere in London is incredible with great support almost along the entire route.

"Having my name on my shirt and a very popular name meant that I got a lot of shouts out – even if they were for another nearby David!"

Capital

Mike Clyne, 44, from Underriver, ran his 12th marathon on the streets of the capital on Sunday and clocked 4hrs 35mins and 11 seconds.

Mr Clyne said: "It was a great day.

"The London Marathon is always a phenomenal day. The support from the crowd was amazing and it really spurred me on.

"Would I have liked to have gone quicker?

"Yes I would, but it did not spoil my day at all.

"I went out for dinner afterwards and had a big steak and my first beer for a few months, and it tasted very good."

Phil Belzar, 29, from Borough Green, ran 5hr 4mins 41 secs. He said: "It was a great day, very hot though, but really enjoyable.

FINISH LINE: Frank Mestre from Kings Hill, who ran the London Marathon on Sunday

"The charity I ran for [Bliss] put on a party afterwards and I had a couple of glasses of champagne, and a few beers too.

"It's nice to know that I can run for enjoyment now rather than for training purposes."

Annette French, from Clenches Farm Lane, Sevenoaks, said: "It was a great day, very hot, but the crowd was great and I had a few glasses of champagne at the end of the day."

Kings Hill's Frank Mestre, a BT Openreach Engineer ran for the National Autism Society and clocked 5hrs 57mins 17secs.

FACT FILE

Frank Mestre, 37, Kings Hill – 5 hours 57 minutes 17 seconds; **Rob Scorey**, 20, Sevenoaks – 4.27.13; **Graham Cook**, Hildenborough – 3.56.53; **Justin Baker**, 39, Godden Green – 4.28.27; **David Hale**, 43, Sevenoaks – 3.17.47; **Phil Belzar**, 29, Borough Green – 5.4.41.

Annette French, 39, Clenches Farm – 4.37.35; **Marius Carboni**, Plaxtol – 4.23.9; **Anna Carboni**, Plaxtol – 4.14.41; **Taricia Brownlie**, 31, Westerham – 5.59.51; **Alice Golding**, Sevenoaks – 4.48.49; **Mike Clyne**, 44, Underriver – 4.35.11.

Runners complete marathon

By Sam Inkersole

THOUSANDS OF RUNNERS for charity joined the world's athletic elite in the London Marathon at the weekend. The ten competitors from the Sevenoaks area who last week featured in the *Chronicle* all managed to complete the gruelling 26.2-mile course.

David Hale timed an impressive 3hrs 17mins 47secs, a personal best for the marathon.

He said: 'It was another scorcher weather-wise.

'At 12 miles, I was on target for 3hrs 10mins.

'I started to feel the quads hurting about 20 miles in but kept my head down and plugged away at what felt like a slow pace but was on a par with everyone around me.

'The atmosphere in London is incredible with great support almost along the entire route.

'Having my name on my shirt and a very popular name meant that I got a lot of shouts out – even if they were for another nearby David!'

Mike Clyne, 44, from Underriver, ran his 12th marathon on the streets of the capital on Sunday and clocked 4hrs 35mins and 11 seconds.

Mr Clyne said: 'It was a great day.

'The London Marathon is always a phenomenal day. The support from the crowd was amazing and it really spurred me on.

'Would I have liked to have gone quicker?

'Yes I would, but it did not spoil my day at all. I went out for dinner afterwards and had a big steak and my first beer for a few months, and it tasted very good.'

Phil Belzar, 29, from Borough Green, ran 5hrs 4mins 41 secs. He said: 'It was a great day, very hot though, but really enjoyable.

'The charity I ran for [Bliss] put on a party afterwards and I had a couple of glasses of champagne, and a few beers too.

'It's nice to know that I can run for enjoyment now rather than for training purposes.'

Annette French, from Clenches Farm Lane, Sevenoaks, said: 'It was a great day, very hot, but the crowd was great and I had a few glasses of champagne at the end of the day.'

Kings Hill's Frank Mestre, a BT Openreach Engineer, ran for the National Autism Society and clocked 5hrs 57mins 17secs.

Duck race cancelled

And Finally...

Dad and child stuck in toilets

A MAN and his child were rescued by fire fighters after being locked in Rock Park's public toilets.

A fire crew from Barnstaple was called to help the pair at lunch time.

The father and child were freed from the toilets next to the play area by fire fighters using small tools.

Dad and child stuck in toilet

A MAN AND his child were rescued by firefighters after being locked in Rock Park's public toilets.

A fire crew from Barnstaple was called to help the pair at lunchtime.

The father and child were freed from the toilets next to the play area by firefighters using small tools.

CAMERA FOUND

A compact camera was found in Station Road on Wednesday afternoon. Any enquiries should be made to Keswick Police Station on 0845 3300247.

Camera found

A COMPACT CAMERA was found in Station Road on Wednesday afternoon. Any enquiries should be made to Keswick Police Station on 0845 3300247.

NEWS IN BRIEF

False alarm

LYME REGIS: Two kayakers sparked an alarm after returning late from a trip between Lyme Regis and West Bay.

The duo turned up shortly afterwards and said that they had been paddling against the tide.

False alarm

LYME REGIS: TWO kayakers sparked an alarm after returning late from a trip between Lyme Regis and West Bay.

The duo turned up shortly afterwards and said that they had been paddling against the tide.

News

www.southlondon-today.co.uk

GIFTS: From left, Muriel Courtney, 12, Joanna Alstott, 11, Savannah Hickey-Ryan, Hannah Arowoselu, 11, and Nanette Boateng, 11

Shoebox gifts for homeless

SCHOOLGIRLS have been filling shoeboxes with gifts to donate to a homeless charity this Christmas.

The girls, from St Ursula's Convent School in Greenwich, filled and decorated the 80 boxes last week ready for delivery to Deptford Churches Centre.

Patricia Muller, director of humanities at St Ursula's, said: "It was all part of our community work.

"The girls have been working with the charity for the last three years, giving gifts, bearing in mind they get so much."

Deptford Churches Centre in Speedwell Street, Deptford, provides a drop-in day centre for vulnerable adults.

Shoebox gifts for homeless

SCHOOLGIRLS HAVE BEEN filling shoeboxes with gifts to donate to a homeless charity this Christmas.

The girls, from St Ursula's Convent School in Greenwich, filled and decorated the 80 boxes last week ready for delivery to Deptford Churches Centre.

Patricia Muller, director of humanities at St Ursula's, said: 'It was all part of our community work.

'The girls have been working with the charity for the last three years, giving gifts, bearing in mind they get so much.'

Deptford Churches Centre in Speedwell Street, Deptford, provides a drop-in day centre for vulnerable adults.

For the record

Zorgon

SANDOWN illuminated procession entry Zorgon was made of bubble wrap and not papier mache and created by Tonya Fisher and Keith French, of Shanklin, and not the Winch family, as reported last week.

The error arose from incorrect information supplied by carnival organisers.

Zorgon

SANDOWN ILLUMINATED PROCESSION entry Zorgon was made of bubble wrap and not papier mâché and created by Tonya Fisher and Keith French, of Shanklin, and not the Winch family, as reported last week.

The error arose from incorrect information supplied by carnival organisers.

Mystery of wheelchair left in Shoreham pub

That pint worked miracles

BEWILDERED BAR STAFF have been left wondering if their beer possesses mystical healing powers after a customer left their wheelchair behind.

It has been languishing in the storeroom of the Crown and Anchor pub in High Street, Shoreham, since it was left behind last November.

Staff recall its elderly owner arrived as part of a group and moved on to a normal chair while he enjoyed a drink.

When the group left, staff discovered the wheelchair was still there.

Owner Dominic Worrall said the incident was like a scene involving characters from BBC comedy *Little Britain*.

He said: 'I think we're looking for Lou and Andy.

'It's a real mystery. Surely when the person left they would have wondered where their wheelchair was?

'Even if they'd had one too many you would have thought they would have come back later to retrieve it.

'Does our Adnams have special healing properties? People generally feel a bit better after a few pints, I suppose.'

Staff have left a note in the window hoping someone will notice and reunite the wheelchair with its mystery owner.

Acknowledgements

THIS BOOK HAS been a labour of love. While it was always supposed to be fun to prod-uce and to read, the intention was never to laugh at the newspapers involved. Rather, *Whitstable Mum in Custard Shortage* is a homage to the craft of journalism, and to the unique qualities of Britain's local press.

Let nobody proclaim the death of local news. Every day there are journalists scouring your local town for news of near accidents, lost animals and bizarre coincidences. These are the stories that make our communities.

Special thanks to: the journalists who gave their time to suggest articles and track down the original pages; the editors who gave their blessing to the book; Roger Kasper, editor of the *Sevenoaks Chronicle* and author of the original 'Whitstable Mum' article; readers of the *Bookseller* magazine who submitted some classic cuttings, particularly Peter Knaggs, Laura Longworth and Jennifer Creswick; researchers Karen Ings, Federico Andornino and Victoria Philpott, who went to extraordinary lengths to track down forgotten copies in dusty archives; Tony Lyons, who laboured to make sure the book's design matched the majesty of it's content; and proofreaders Shan Morley Jones and Sarah Coward.

The Penguins who made it possible include Katie Alton, Stuart Anderson, Dave Atkinson, Sita Balani, Roseanne Bantick, Claire Bennett, Gemma Blackman, Venetia Butterfield, Tom Chicken, Matt Clacher, Caroline Craig, Jane Delaney, Anna Derkacz, David Devaney, Helen Eka, Alex Elam, Helen Evans, John Faiers, Amelia Fairney, Charlie Gardner, Neil Green, John Hamilton, Ross Hulbert, Doulglas Neely, Sophie Overment, Jon Parker, Carl Rolfe, Richard Screech, Katya Shipster, Carolyn Smith, Ellie Smith and Phil Twomey.

If you've spotted a local story that deserves to be included in the next edition, please email joel.rickett@uk.penguingroup.com or tweet #WhitstableMum, or even write to me at Penguin Group (UK), 80 Strand, London WC2R 0RL.

Happy custard hunting.

Joel Rickett
Editorial Director, Viking

List of Headlines

List of Newspapers

MUM IN CUSTARD SHORTAGE

making **local** matter **more**   Established 1863

WHITSTABLE
TIMES

visit our website
www.thisiskent.co.uk